The Cameroon War

SOUTHERN
QUESTIONS

Decolonisation was the major historical process of the twentieth century. Its unfinished projects continue to shape our present. The defeat, withdrawal and reconfiguration of Western colonial power in the postwar decades have affected almost everyone alive today, with stunning unevenness. The Southern Questions series features first-hand accounts – memoirs, novels, pamphlets – written by participants in the drama of decolonisation and its aftermath. Alongside these titles, Southern Questions presents new histories, reportage and literary criticism devoted to nations, regions and zones in the South.

Adom Getachew
Thomas Meaney
Series Editors

Titles in this series from Verso Books:

Everybody Loves a Good Drought by Palagummi Sainath

Literature at the End of History by Pankaj Mishra

My Country, Africa by Andrée Blouin

This Fiction Called Nigeria by Adéwálé Májà-Pearce

The Cameroon War

*A History of French
Neocolonialism in Africa*

By Thomas Deltombe, Manuel
Domergue and Jacob Tatsitsa

Translated by David Broder

VERSO

London • New York

This English-language edition first published by Verso 2025
Originally published as *La Guerre du Cameroun. L'invention de la Françafrique 1948–1971*
© Éditions La Découverte 2016
Translation © David Broder 2025

The manufacturer's authorised representative in the EU for product safety
(GPSR) is LOGOS EUROPE, 9 rue Nicolas Poussin, 17000, La Rochelle, France
contact@logoseurope.eu

1 3 5 7 9 10 8 6 4 2

Verso
UK: 6 Meard Street, London W1F 0EG
US: 207 32nd Street, New York, NY 10016
versobooks.com

Verso is the imprint of New Left Books

ISBN-13: 978-1-78873-376-2
ISBN-13: 978-1-78873-378-6 (UK EBK)
ISBN-13: 978-1-78873-379-3 (US EBK)

British Library Cataloguing in Publication Data
A catalogue record for this book is available from the British Library

Library of Congress Cataloging-in-Publication Data

Names: Deltombe, Thomas author | Tatsitsa, Jacob author | Domergue, Manuel,
1981– author
Title: The Cameroon war : a history of French neocolonialism in Africa / by
Thomas Deltombe, Jacob Tatsitsa and Manuel Domergue ; translated by
David Broder.
Other titles: Guerre du Cameroun. English
Description: First edition paperback. | London ; New York : Verso Books,
2025. | Series: Southern questions | 'Originally published as La guerre
du Cameroun. L'invention de la Françafrique 1948–1971 <div>© Éditions
La Découverte 2016' – Title page verso. | Includes bibliographical
references and index.
Identifiers: LCCN 2025004414 (print) | LCCN 2025004415 (ebook) | ISBN
9781788733762 paperback | ISBN 9781788733793 ebk
Subjects: LCSH: National liberation movements – Cameroon |
Insurgency – Cameroon – History – 20th century |
Decolonization – Cameroon – History | Cameroon – History – Autonomy and
independence movements | Cameroon – Relations – France – History |
France – Relations – Cameroon – History | Cameroon – Politics and
government – 20th century | France – Politics and government – 20th century
| France – Colonies – Africa – Administration
Classification: LCC DT573.5.F8 D4513 2025 (print) | LCC DT573.5.F8
(ebook) | DDC 967.11/03 – dc23/eng/20250312
LC record available at https://lccn.loc.gov/2025004414
LC ebook record available at https://lccn.loc.gov/2025004415

Typeset in Fournier by Biblichor Ltd, Scotland
Printed and bound by CPI Group (UK) Ltd, Croydon CR0 4YY

Contents

Africa in the early 1950s

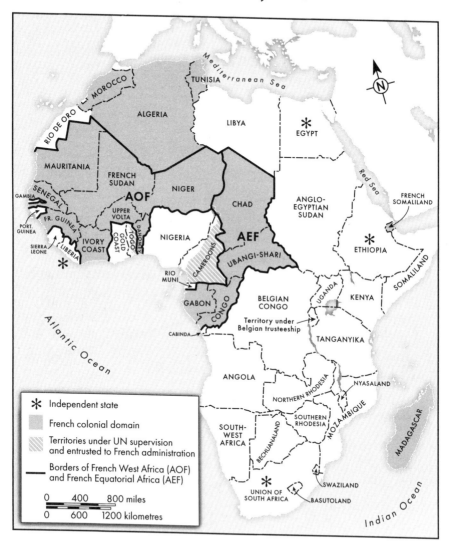

MOROCCO
RIO DE ORO
TUNISIA
Mediterranean Sea
ALGERIA
LIBYA
EGYPT ✳
MAURITANIA
FRENCH SUDAN
NIGER
CHAD
Red Sea
ANGLO-EGYPTIAN SUDAN
FRENCH SOMALILAND
AOF
GAMBIA
SENEGAL
PORT. GUINEA
FR. GUINEA
UPPER VOLTA
GOLD COAST
TOGO
DAHOMEY
NIGERIA
AEF
UBANGI-SHARI
ETHIOPIA ✳
SIERRA LEONE
LIBERIA
IVORY COAST
✳
CAMEROONS
RIO MUNI
SOMALILAND
GABON
CONGO
BELGIAN CONGO
UGANDA
KENYA
CABINDA
Territory under Belgian trusteeship
TANGANYIKA
Atlantic Ocean
ANGOLA
NORTHERN RHODESIA
NYASALAND
SOUTH-WEST AFRICA
SOUTHERN RHODESIA
MOZAMBIQUE
MADAGASCAR
BECHUANALAND
UNION OF SOUTH AFRICA
SWAZILAND
BASUTOLAND
Indian Ocean

N

✳ Independent state
  French colonial domain
  Territories under UN supervision and entrusted to French administration
  Borders of French West Africa (AOF) and French Equatorial Africa (AEF)

0   400   800 miles
0   600   1200 kilometres

Cameroon under French and British administrations in the mid-1950s

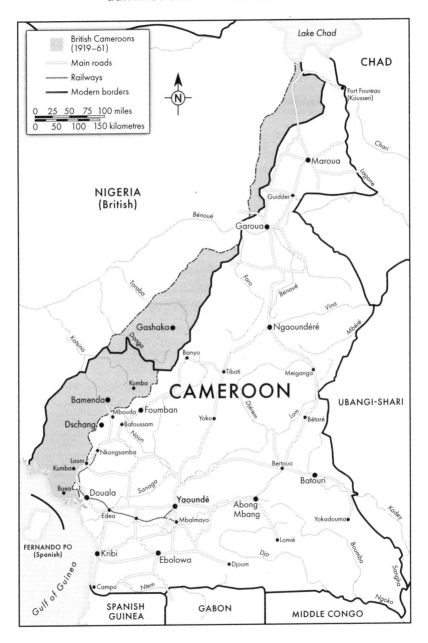

British Cameroons
(1919–61)
Main roads
Railways
Modern borders

0 25 50 75 100 miles
0   50 100 150 kilometres

N

Lake Chad

CHAD

Fort Foureau
(Kousseri)

Chari

NIGERIA
(British)

Maroua

Guidder

Bénoué

Garoua

Logone

Taraba

Faro

Bénoué

Vina

Mbéré

Gashaka

Donga

Banyo

Ngaoundéré

UBANGI-SHARI

Kumbo

Tibati

Meiganga

Bamenda

Mbouda

Foumban

CAMEROON

Yoko

Diérem

Lom

Bétaré

Dschang

Bafoussam

Noun

Nkongsamba

Katsina

Loum

Bertoua

Kumba

Batouri

Kodey

Buea

Douala

Sanaga

Yaoundé

Abong
Mbang

Yokadouma

Edéa

Mbalmayo

Lomié

Boumba

FERNANDO PO
(Spanish)

Kribi

Ebolowa

Djoum

Dja

Sangha

Gulf of Guinea

Campo

Ntem

SPANISH
GUINEA

GABON

MIDDLE CONGO

Ngoko

Source: L'Exportateur français, 1 March 1952, and *Report of the British Authorities to
the United Nations General Assembly on the Administration of Cameroon under British
Trusteeship for the Year 1952*, London, HMSO, 1953.

Introduction: An Invisible War

*Psychological warfare is not 'declared'. It does not 'break out',
accompanied by spectacular measures like mass mobilisation and
the mustering of armies. It takes hold, it 'is there'; one fine day,
you realise that it is raging with some intensity, and the terrible
thing is that by the time its victims come to realise this, it is usually
already too late. Psychological warfare is secret; it is, above all
else, clandestine.*

— Major Jean Lamberton, *La Guerre psychologique*,
École d'état-major, 1954–55

Meeting a ghost is no ordinary experience. For years, we'd been
trying to track down the man who co-authored *OK cargo!*, published
in 1988 and subtitled *A Helicopter Pilot's Saga in Africa*. This was a
strange book, full of spectres, corpses and obscure pseudonyms. Telling the story – the back cover put it – of 'twenty white-hot years of
adventure, or total war', the pilot even dedicated a chapter to a 'genocide' in which he claimed to have taken part in Cameroon after that
country's independence in 1960.

Unlike most of the French witnesses whom we had met through our
long investigation into this little-known war, described in detail in our
Kamerun![1] – the 2011 study to which the book in your hands is at once
a synthesis and a sequel – the author did not hold back. 'In two years,'
he wrote, 'the regular army occupied the Bamileke region, from north
to south, and completely devastated it. They massacred 300,000 or

400,000 Bamileke. A true genocide. They practically annihilated the race . . . The villages had been razed to the ground, a bit like Attila: you passed through and nothing was left standing. Few Frenchmen intervened directly. I only knew three or four of them, that was it. The press did not mention it.'[2]

The pilot Max Bardet's philosophy of massacres

So, we tried to find out more about this helicopter pilot. His book's publisher in Paris, Éditions Grasset, wasn't especially cooperative. Its answer basically went, 'It's an old book, and the man you are looking for may well be dead.' His co-author, a certain Nina Thellier, who had helped him complete the manuscript, was likewise impossible to find. Presented in the book as an 'American businesswoman', press attaché at the Paris-Dakar Rally and 'executive director of a Paris PR firm', she seemed to have disappeared without trace.

We had also contacted another man, Constantin Melnik (1927–2014). Chief of intelligence at the Hôtel Matignon – the French prime minister's office – from 1959 to 1962, and at the time the great rival of General de Gaulle's powerful adviser Jacques Foccart, Melnik later specialised in *romans à clef*, producing a number of books in which he recounted his past exploits in a fine-tuned blend of fact and fiction. It was Melnik, as a series editor at Éditions Grasset, who had published *OK cargo!* But Melnik kept his silence, and we began to question the very existence of the helicopter pilot whose named appeared nowhere in the myriad military archives that we had consulted. What did the jacket copy really mean when it described him as 'legendary'?

Some time after the publication of our investigation, in which we mentioned this mysterious pilot, a reader wrote to inform us that the story of Max Bardet – so he was called – was less of a 'legend' than we might have imagined. The writer of the letter had carried out '[his] military service at Air Base 174 in Douala, Cameroon, in 1963–64', and so had known Bardet 'well'. Passionate about Cameroon, where he had lived from 1957 to 1965, our reader nonetheless took a certain critical distance from *OK cargo!*: 'The death toll claimed by Staff Sergeant Bardet is staggering but implausible.'

All the same, the ghost did exist. He even picked up the telephone. Bardet readily agreed to meet with us at his home, in the suburbs of Albi, one day in summer 2014. Yet his account did not exactly clear up the mystery. While Bardet was keen to cast his African adventures in epic tones, he left countless details unexplained. For instance, the identities of his protagonists – referred to by pseudonyms in the book – were irretrievably lost. 'I deliberately forgot all their names,' he told us. 'I forgot them, it's no joke. I'm not lying to you. I forgot them. I saw too many things, I did too many things, I heard about too many things.'

But what did Max Bardet see, and do, in Cameroon? After hours of interviews with him, it is still difficult to answer with any certainty. His way of telling the story is to pile up a vast mélange of known facts, plausible claims, unverifiable allegations, traumatic recollections, lapses of memory and simple bragging. All of this is peppered with contradictions and telling silences. But still, we have to try to examine his story more closely.

Bardet was, most crucially, a lost soldier of the Algerian War. Close to the Organisation armée secrète (OAS), to which he loaned his car for night-time racist 'rat hunts' in Algiers, he was transferred to Cameroon in 1962 by way of punishment. Considered an 'undesirable element' by then armed forces minister Pierre Messmer, he was assigned to Douala, Cameroon's economic capital. On the fringes of the fighting units, he was placed under the intermittent authority of a mysterious captain whom he calls 'Leroy' in the book, but whose real name he claims to have forgotten. The captain clearly didn't want attention, Bardet points out: 'Perhaps he was an intelligence guy, or who knows what.'

After his years fighting in Algeria, life in Douala seemed awfully placid to this adventurer with a hunger for bold feats and grand gestures. 'The war was over,' he writes – alluding to the terrible events that had preceded his arrival in Cameroon of which he apparently knew almost nothing. 'We could go out on the town. With my wife, we went dancing in nightclubs, everyone got along, it was great; we lived as if we were back home.' But while the mood remained the same in Douala, in 1963 the nature of Bardet's activities as a pilot, which had at first consisted of transporting French officers, changed dramatically: 'All of a sudden, the captain revealed to me that the war was there, that it was still underway.'

Bardet now embarked on secret operations in western Cameroon, otherwise known as the Bamileke region, an area of rolling hills around a hundred kilometres from Douala. Even now, he has only the vaguest idea of what the political situation in Cameroon was at the time. That subject was of little interest to him. But he describes in detail the 'massacres' in which he took part.

The story he tells us is a catalogue of horrors, whose darkest episodes are absent from his book. He describes, for example, vast operations against rebel villages over the course of 1963. African troops loyal to the government, drunk on palm wine, cleared the huts with extraordinary violence. 'They killed everyone, women, children . . . The men, at least, they shot with Kalashnikovs. But the women they killed, they cut off their breasts, they disembowelled them, especially pregnant women.' What did the pilot do while this was taking place? He flew over the area, ensuring that no one could escape: 'The guy next to you at the radio says, "Two getting away to the northeast." Pow, the sound of a Jeep, two bursts of a machine gun.' What were they trying to avoid? That anyone who escaped would 'tell the story of what was happening', he explained. Bardet claims to have taken part in such operations three times. These 'controlled massacres', as he calls them, supposedly killed almost 1,500 people.

The pilot also tells us about the practice of 'offloading', or dumping the bodies of the recently murdered in rivers: 'When I first heard about it, I didn't believe it. I was told, "It's no big deal, when something goes down, we dump them in the Noun, with trucks." I said, "No, you're kidding . . ." "You'll see, in the Noun valley, the river is white with the bones of the dead." And that's what I saw, hundreds and hundreds of corpses. But all that was left were the bones. I thought, "Damn, it's true."'

The striking thing in Bardet's story is that he seems to have developed a sort of philosophy of massacres. He distinguishes between two varieties of collective killings, depending on the method used: 'It's one thing to massacre people, when you massacre them, how to put it, cleanly. You shoot them with a Kalashnikov or a machine gun, you line them up – rat-a-tat. They're dead, they're dead. But when you massacre people with machetes, for the thrill of it . . . for the thrill, huh? They wanted to do it, I don't know why, what could that have done for them? To go and cut off the feet of a guy who's dead already, what's that really doing for you?' So, there were civilised massacres and uncivilised ones . . .

Bardet doesn't tell us in which category he places a practice beloved of his captain: the use of phosphorous grenades, thrown from the helicopter onto the fleeing guerrillas. But it wasn't hard to guess when we heard him describe the burnt corpses of the victims, whose faces could still be identified: 'Perfectly done!'

Beyond 'tribal violence', the real causes of the war

We could fill many pages narrating Bardet's dazzling 'adventures'. Indeed, this is what he did in *OK cargo!* But we would do better to steer well clear of that. Not only is it difficult to corroborate the facts – secret massacres, coordinated by an anonymous captain, that left no witnesses – but the pilot's narrative conceals as much as it reveals. In his philosophy of massacres, Bardet does not appear to have given any consideration to the Cameroonian political context in which he was operating. His account simply speaks of France's desire to stop 'Communists' putting down roots in Cameroon. Described in its everyday routine, the war seems to boil down to a simple clash of irrational 'ethnic rivalries'.

Seven years after he published Bardet's book, Constantin Melnik authored his own *La Mort était leur mission* (Their Mission Was Death), in which he talks about Cameroon. This semi-fictional novel, which is full of half-invented characters, likewise interprets the conflict in terms of ethnic rivalries:

> After the decolonisation orchestrated by General de Gaulle, unrest broke out in Cameroon. Where was this damn country, anyway? What was its history and what made it unique? An extremist Bamileke faction had risen up in rebellion. Following an African tradition, not yet relayed on TV, there was a series of massacres, followed by a crackdown in which the government forces, backed by French military advisors, showed little restraint. Enticed by African adventure . . . Colonel Martineau's comrades had set out to fly helicopters and they returned full of tales of corpses floating downstream or rotting in the forests.[3]

It's a well-worn habit: reducing all conflicts in Africa to tribal clashes and describing them as a mere succession of massacres. This allows for the political causes to be erased, the names of those responsible to be spirited away, and the victims blamed for the violence committed against them. Who started this war in Cameroon? Who organised it? Who profited from it? The presence of a French helicopter pilot, fluttering around above the 'controlled massacres', alone proves that this was not simply a matter of ethnic killings.

The acts of violence described by Bardet, Melnik and many others are quite obviously very important, if only because of the individual and collective traumas that resulted. But to reduce the Cameroon War to a series of massacres is to give up on any hope of understanding its logic. Hypnotised by the terrible consequences, we end up forgetting their causes. Captivated by the flash of machetes, we silently absolve the criminals lurking in the shadows. For not only was the crime the moment of the massacres: it also implicates the executioners in suits and ties who made those massacres possible.

This is what we illustrate over the pages that follow, through a political and historical analysis of the Cameroon War. Of course, the bid to move beyond narrowly ethnic interpretations does not mean ignoring the local dynamics of the conflict and its endogenous logics. Rather, it means grasping how these factors, which were also historically and politically situated, fit into a wider, more intricate battle for domination. We will then see how even partly autonomous, local logics are sometimes weaponised and reinvented to suit outside interests.

There is something obscene about Melnik's *roman à clef*, when it lays all the blame on 'African traditions', dates the unrest to 'after' independence, and explains that repression 'followed' the massacres. Melnik knew that all this was untrue. As coordinator of the secret services at the prime minister's office from 1959 to 1962, he was perfectly familiar with the reality; when Cameroon became independent on 1 January 1960, this delicate dossier had been taken from the Ministry of French Overseas Territories and entrusted to Matignon itself.

Melnik was thus well aware that the supposed ethnic conflict that had raged through Cameroon did not result from the independence granted by France but was – as we will see in Chapter One – rooted in a much older history. Its origins date back to the colonial conquest of the country, occupied by Germany at the end of the nineteenth century and carved up between the British and French after the First World War. The internal tensions that surfaced as Cameroon prepared for independence were the result of colonial policy. And it was the French desire first to avoid; then to delay; and finally, for want of a better alternative, to 'supervise' that independence, to void it of substance – in short, to prevent Cameroonians from freely determining their future – that would poison the situation in the 1950s.

France's enemy in these years of decolonisation was not ethnic, but political: the Union des populations du Cameroon (UPC), the independence movement founded in 1948 that stubbornly refused to allow France to impose its choices on Cameroon (Chapter Two). This refusal was all the more obstinate because the Cameroonian nationalists knew that both their country's legal status and international law worked to their advantage. Cameroon, provisionally declared a League of Nations mandate at the end of the First World War because it was judged unfit for independence – just like Syria, Lebanon, Palestine, Togo, Rwanda and other German and Ottoman territories – had only temporarily been placed under British and French authority. London and Paris signed international agreements promising to shepherd the territories they administered towards autonomy or independence.

Precisely because international law was not on their side, the French authorities chose to use force to get their way (Chapter Three). Of course, the war launched against the UPC in the 1950s would subsequently take on an 'ethnic' character, even if its main target in fact changed over time: the 'Bassa' of the Sanaga-Maritime from 1956 to 1958, and then the 'Bamileke' of western Cameroon. But this ethnicisation of the conflict was only a ploy, a diversion and a means of warfare aimed at dividing the Cameroonian national movement.

In this historical context, the purportedly 'ethnic' war, sometimes described as a Cameroonian 'civil war', concealed eminently political interests. The focus on ethnicity also obscures the geopolitical stakes of the war (see Chapter Four). Indeed, after having installed a pro-French regime in Yaoundé, France did not only seek to crush its Cameroonian opponents, whatever their supposed ethnic identity. This was the era of the Cold War, and France also claimed to be defending the regime against the Communist powers, who were accused of being the hand behind the 'rebels'. Less officially, France was also wary of the British and Americans – anti-Communist allies but rival imperial powers – who were suspected of wanting to exploit potential chaos in order to get a foothold in the newly independent country. Behind these multiple adversaries, which were sometimes raised as mere pretexts, Paris sought above all to keep Cameroon in its orbit and to perpetuate its dominance in Africa, despite the seditious winds of decolonisation. In this regard, the Cameroon War played a central role in the emergence of a new type of semi-official, semi-informal neocolonial governance, which would later be called 'Françafrique' (Chapter Five).

'Counterrevolutionary warfare', or the logic of eradication

Despite his preference for casting the conflict in tribal terms, Bardet did get one thing right: it really was a war. Having 'done Algeria' and taken part in a fair number of other conflicts afterwards, he knew what he was talking about. The term *war*, which was never officially used, appears repeatedly in confidential reports by French soldiers who participated in the operations. In 1957, General Louis Dio, armed forces commander for the French Equatorial Africa (AEF)–Cameroon defence zone, held that the battles in Cameroon 'no longer constitute an operation to restore order, but a "war operation"'.[4] The next year, a battalion leader wrote, 'The awareness that we are indeed at war allowed for considerable results to be achieved.'[5] In 1960, General Max Briand, who directed military operations, spoke of a 'phenomenon of subversive warfare'.[6]

There was then no doubt that this conflict was indeed a 'war'. This was obvious to the French soldiers, to their Cameroonian allies and to their enemies hiding in the *maquis*. The fact remains that the notion of 'war' is equivocal, insofar as it has a rather porous border separating it from 'politics'. For Carl von Clausewitz, 'War is the continuation of politics by other means,' though eminent philosophers have since retorted that it is more like the other way around. Whatever the case, this question is posed especially sharply in the colonial context. 'The colonial situation is first of all a military conquest continued and reinforced by a civil and police administration,' wrote the Martinican psychiatrist Frantz Fanon, who gave his support to Algeria's National Liberation Front (FLN), adding 'French colonialism is a war force.'[7]

If colonialism is a permanent state of exception, which does not refrain even from massacres in order to conquer territory and impose its law, how can it be distinguished from war as such? This ambiguity explains in part why the French, so accustomed to 'maintaining order' by violent methods, thought for so long that they could describe the Algerian War as simple 'events'.

The situation in Cameroon was more complicated. There, the war was not prompted by an insurrection comparable to the Algerian 'Toussaint rouge' of 1 November 1954. Nor was it brought to an end by the signing of an official document comparable to the Evian Accords of 18 March 1962. The Cameroon War began quietly in the 1950s, tensions rose bit by bit from the moment of independence, and the insurrection survived through the 1960s before petering out at the turn of the 1970s. The eventual victory of the French and their allies (unlike in Algeria) and the installation of a ruthless dictatorship in Yaoundé – that is to say, the continuation of war by other means – not only relegated the conflict to the status of mere 'unrest' but finally erased it from official memory (Chapter Six). These circumstances make it hard to tell when the war started and when it was over. If a war has no beginning or end, did it ever take place?

But what allow us nonetheless to speak of a war are the methods used by the French authorities. As in Algeria at the same time, in Cameroon the French army deployed the novel, visionary techniques of what is known today as the 'doctrine of revolutionary warfare'

(DRW). This doctrine is characterised precisely by its blurring of the boundary between war and politics. Inspired by the combined civil-military approach of veteran colonial officers (Hubert Lyautey and Joseph Gallieni), the psychological warfare pioneered by British and American soldiers, and by Viet Minh tactics during the First Indochina War (1946–54), DRW became a preferred instrument of French strategists in the 1950s. Defeated at Diên Biên Phu in May 1954 and having faced all-out rebellion in Algeria just six months later, these officers became fixated on crushing any further anticolonial insurrection in the egg. This was the scenario that played out in Cameroon from 1955 onwards: the French authorities decided to eradicate the Cameroonian nationalist movement, suddenly regarded as a new Viet Minh. With the banning of the UPC, the political opposition was turned into a military enemy.

The Cameroon War thus finds its place in a long history of counter-insurgency or counter-subversion campaigns. It is a history that stretches far beyond Franco-Cameroonian relations, beginning in the immediate aftermath of the Second World War and continuing on to today's anti-terrorist wars. Breaking with the classic Clausewitzian schema, these wars are aimed less at destroying the enemy on the frontlines and more at controlling the rear, which is to say the population itself. 'The number one problem', one of the leading French counterinsurgency theorists, Colonel Charles Lacheroy (1906–2005), explained in 1954, 'is establishing a grip over the populations that act as a support base for this war and in the midst of whom it is waged. Whoever takes charge of them and keeps control of them has won already.'[8]

What Lacheroy called 'revolutionary warfare' – better described as counterrevolutionary warfare – is a political war aimed at destroying, in an expression borrowed from Mao Zedong, the subversive fish by attacking them in the water through which they swim: the people. To this end, countless mechanisms of bodily, territorial and psychological control are enlisted in order to establish a grip over the civilian population, isolate the enemy elements, force them to defend themselves against the 'subversive contagion', and finally to win their hearts and minds. All manner of such tools were used on a greater or lesser scale in Cameroon in the 1950s and 1960s. They included the identification of individuals, the introduction of permits to move around, the installation of checkpoints, the creation of 'resettlement camps', the deportation of populations, the establishment of 'pacification zones', the recruitment of militias, aerial bombardments, targeted assassinations, forced disappearances, public executions, the exhibition of decapitated heads, systematic torture, psychological manipulation and brainwashing.

A terrible human toll

How many lives did the Cameroon War claim? Tens of thousands? One hundred thousand? It is unlikely we will ever know with any certainty. According to a confidential report by General Max Briand, commander of the French forces in Cameroon in the early postindependence years, the human toll of the fighting in the Bamileke region in 1960 alone amounted to 'a little more than 20,000 men'. Of these, a reported 5,000 died in combat, 1,000 from their wounds, 5,000 fell victim to disease, and 10,000 – the lion's share of them – were killed in a vaguely defined 'internal struggle'. On the side of the forces of order, across all units there were 614 'allied casualties' including 583 African civilians.[9]

Much more complete and convincing than this partial and biased accounting, the British embassy, present in the vicinity and with a good knowledge of the situation on the ground, also attempted to establish the human cost in a confidential report written in 1964. 'The estimated civilian casualties between January 1956 and June 1, 1962 . . . are said to be between 60,000 and 75,000 dead.'[10] At a talk in October 1962, *Le Monde*'s André Blanchet — a journalist well versed in Cameroonian affairs who was close to French authorities — quoted a source worth 'taking seriously' to the effect that there were 'a total of 120,000 victims during the two or three years that the insurrection lasted in the [Bamileke] country'.[11] This figure does not count the toll of the 'unrest' in other regions, particularly in the Sanaga-Maritime between 1955 and 1958.

These — very rough — attempts to count the numbers also exclude the thousands of people who perished as a result of the appalling living conditions in the resettlement camps in the Sanaga-Maritime and in the Bamileke region. A thorough count of the Cameroon War death toll would also have to include those who died behind closed doors during Ahmadou Ahidjo's dictatorship in the 1960s and 1970s — those who fell victim to internment camps, torture, disappearances and public and extra-judicial executions and have never been tallied.

The human cost of the Cameroon War is all the harder to establish because DRW dissolves the boundaries between soldiers and civilians, sympathisers and belligerents. The bombings, for example, were aimed at no-go zones, and the people living there were considered hostile by definition. Orders were given to 'annihilate' both insurgents 'and their sympathisers'.

The fact that the Cameroon War was outsourced, ethnicised and concealed made it all the crueller. The combination of elements of classic warfare and certain elements of civil war — designed by the French army to subcontract and camouflage its repression — makes it very difficult to draw up a balance sheet, in the absence of impartial observers on the ground at the time. But we do know one thing for sure: the conflict resulted in at least tens of thousands of deaths, and possibly many more. 'After the war we stop counting the dead,' goes the Bamileke proverb.[12]

While these tactics surely allow for comparisons between Cameroon and Algeria, where the same methods were employed at the same time, this is no exclusively French phenomenon. Indeed, Cameroon could also be compared to a British colony, Kenya, where in the 1950s the imperial authorities pursued a similar policy to eliminate the Mau Mau movement. In certain respects, the Cameroon War might also be seen alongside what happened thirty years later in Rwanda, where the French-backed 'Hutu power' used techniques derived from DRW to methodically eliminate the Tutsis.

These parallels are worth considering insofar as they underline the totalitarian nature of the doctrines developed by Western armed forces in the context of both decolonisation and the Cold War. These doctrines were fundamentally anti-democratic – by the express admission of Lacheroy, who recognised that his methods were 'revolting to the human conscience' – and aimed at definitively eradicating the enemy, be it Communist, nationalist, 'ethnic, or all of them at once'.[13] Still, this policy could take different forms and reach various degrees of radicalism (involving ideological, political or physical elimination), and it did not always achieve its intended results. Hence the difficulty of naming these processes and the variety of terms used to try to classify them (politicide, sociocide, ethnocide, genocide, democide and so on). But what can be said with more confidence is that the intensive application of counter-subversion doctrines in Cameroon had lasting consequences that are still visible today, well beyond its borders.

Africa under control – and silence as a weapon

If we want to really understand the effect of these military doctrines, it is also important to consider their economic dimension. It is perhaps surprising that the French authorities could extirpate their Cameroonian enemies even while using such modest human or financial resources. But there is an explanation for this in the nature of DRW itself: namely, in its focus on mobilising the population. Relying massively on local forces, and seeking to actively involve civilians in the struggle, France especially emphasised the various hierarchies – be they police, administrative, military or paramilitary commands – that allowed it to 'take charge of the masses'. This partial outsourcing of the repressive effort made it possible not only to 'establish a grip' over the population, to use Lacheroy's vocabulary, but also to save resources already stretched thin in other theatres (starting with Algeria).

As the war progressed after Cameroonian independence, the doctrine developed by French officers gradually mutated into a means of governance. Set at the heart of what political scientists call state-building, *counter-subversive warfare* gave birth to a *counter-subversive state*. For the Cameroonian leaders to whom Paris had in part subcontracted the tasks of maintaining order (while closely controlling them), 'establishing a grip' over the population became an obsession. State and para-state institutions were created out of this same determination to suppress all forms of opposition. Hence the building of a ruthless, ultra-centralised dictatorship in Yaoundé – a regime equipped with a single political party, an omnipresent army and formidable secret police. Paris considered the Cameroonian system an efficient model, and it would be exported to the other French colonies in Africa when they gained their independence. By keeping former French Africa under control, despite its formal independence, the neocolonialism of Françafrique took on a stridently counter-subversive character.

It is striking that DRW ultimately aims to uproot any political will, however slight, among the people, which is suspected of harbouring subversive elements. To return to the Maoist metaphor, we might say that the water was frozen in order to asphyxiate the fish. Colonisation had sought to exclude the natives from politics, and Africans were viewed as objects that could be destroyed, animals who should be trained or children that needed firm leadership. The essence of neocolonialism was to perpetuate this habit: the African, forever immature, must not venture into politics. And yet, explained Ruben Um Nyobè, the historic first leader of the Cameroonian nationalist movement: 'Everything is political and everything involves politics. To say that you don't do politics is to admit that you have no desire to live.'[14] The French war machine aimed precisely at annihilating that desire to live.

Why have we never heard about this war? The question is often posed to researchers and journalists who work on these questions, and there are several possible answers.

In part, the silence surrounding the unrest that afflicted Cameroon is owed to the particular legal status of this territory, which had been placed under an international mandate. Although the trustee powers were meant to be accountable to the United Nations, France concealed its military operations, in contravention of its treaty commitments. Everything was done to demonstrate to the international community and indeed to the domestic public that Paris was governing Cameroon peacefully, with the consent of the local populations. 'Silence must reign,' insisted Colonel Jean Lamberton, military chief of the Sanaga-Maritime Pacification Zone, in 1958.

The silence was all the more deafening given that in this same period France was being criticised for its handling of the Algerian crisis. Monopolising attention, the Algerian War – which mobilised hundreds of thousands of French troops and daily made front-page news – overshadowed the events taking place simultaneously in Cameroon, a much more distant colony of considerably less strategic importance than Algeria. The relatively limited forces deployed in Cameroon also help explain why metropolitan France devoted such little attention to this conflict. Seeing as France relied on Cameroonian auxiliaries and troops from its other colonies (Chad, Gabon, Côte d'Ivoire), few French soldiers saw action in Cameroon and only a handful lost their lives.

French authorities' chosen casting of the conflict as a series of ethnic clashes also played a role in the general disinterest in the Cameroonian unrest. The few observers who were paying attention thus tended to portray the conflict as a grim case of 'the same old negro business'. Meanwhile, labelling the pro-independence forces 'Communists' was sufficient to quieten France's allies abroad, starting with the British. The British archives show that London was perfectly well informed about what was happening on the other side of the border that separated the two Cameroonian mandate territories. But it preferred to cooperate with Paris in the counter-subversive struggle rather than denounce the atrocities in the French zone.

The silence became even louder after the independence of French Cameroon. Now freed from UN oversight, and in a moment when the Algerian War was coming to an end, France carried out its military operations with the greatest discretion, taking care to note that they were conducted 'at the request of the Cameroonian government'. Faithful to its moral obligations – or so it claimed – the former trustee power was only 'helping' the new-found Cameroonian state to relieve the 'tensions' that had come with independence.

As demonstrated by the testimony of Bardet, whose flight logs never detailed the missions in question, the methods used in this framework of 'technical assistance' were carefully kept secret. 'Ultimately, the line in Cameroon was the "three wise monkeys": nothing seen, nothing heard,' the former helicopter pilot recounted. 'When I was taken back to Yaoundé, I was told to forget what I'd seen, that it had never happened. I was told: "Listen, you're going to promise you'll never speak of what you've seen, because it would be a little shaming for France."'

In this transitional period, the Yaoundé regime also sought to keep quiet about its handling of opponents. Aware that they owed everything to French cooperation, the Cameroonian leaders silenced anyone who might have challenged their legitimacy. Those who continued the underground struggle were killed – or rather, to use a term used by a number of witnesses, 'erased'. The others fell victim to the anti-subversive laws passed at the beginning of the 1960s, a legal pretext used by the political police to dispatch 'suspects' to 'administrative internment camps'. Simply mentioning the name of a pro-independence leader could earn you long torture sessions.

The imposition of silence thus had a privileged role within the arsenal of counter-subversion techniques. While censorship and propaganda muted the roar of weapons and the cries of the tortured, the geographic isolation of the 'infested zones' could delude even those who lived only a few dozen kilometres away into thinking that the rebellion had been definitively crushed. 'Given the localised character of the rebellion, it was entirely possible to travel to Cameroon and even to the capital, Yaoundé, without ever suspecting that some regions were drenched in blood, or that people were being killed every day.' So explained, some years later, *Le Monde*'s André Blanchet, a journalist who had himself abundantly relayed French propaganda at the height of the conflict.[15]

The veil of silence that fell over Cameroon was accompanied by painstaking control over the information circulated in France. The Cameroonian writer Mongo Beti experienced this in 1972, when Éditions Maspero published his book *Main basse sur le Cameroun*. A devastating indictment of the activities of France and its Cameroonian allies, this remarkable book was immediately banned and the copies were seized by French authorities. While they were at it, they harassed the author by questioning his dual citizenship and thereby threatening possible extradition. After several years fighting in the courts, Mongo Beti would at last see his work appear, and thus attempt, as he explained, to smash France's 'most formidable weapon' in Africa, 'silence, whose implacable law strangled the Cameroonian people, with no recourse'.[16]

Defying amnesia

The American historian Caroline Elkins refers to the silence that followed the British repression of the Mau Mau in Kenya as an instance of 'state-imposed amnesia'. The line likewise applies to Cameroon: everything was done so that this invisible war would never return to haunt official French memory. This organised amnesia has led to some surprising, or at least telling, episodes. When French prime minister François Fillon visited Yaoundé in May 2009, a journalist asked him about the French responsibility for the assassination of Cameroonian nationalist leaders. He astonishingly replied, in a mixture of ignorance and contempt: 'I totally deny that French participated in any way in assassinations in Cameroon. All that is pure invention!'

But ghosts are in the habit of coming back to haunt us. For some years now, a new generation of Cameroonian historians has been leafing through the archives and travelling up and down Cameroon to interview the last survivors. This is a race against the clock, as the archives, poorly preserved, rot quickly in the country's tropical climate. As for eyewitnesses, there are ever fewer of them in a country where the average life expectancy is just fifty-five. This is, then, a tough job. It is also a courageous one: the war remains an extremely sensitive subject for the Cameroonian regime. It is today led – as it has been since 1982 – by the ultra-authoritarian nonagenarian Paul Biya, direct heir to Ahmadou Ahidjo (1924–89), the dictator installed by France upon independence. Nonetheless, associations bringing together nationalist veterans, historians and activists are working to uncover buried memories.

In France, too, some people have set out to collect the available archives and find surviving eyewitnesses. Books have been published, and a few documentaries made. In the months that followed the publication of our book *Kamerun!* in 2011, two MPs questioned the successive governments of both the right and left as to the French state's official position on the Cameroon War. The answers were shameful, in both cases. Ignoring the work done for years by Cameroonian, French and American researchers, the response was the same both times: 'The period in question belongs to history' and 'Now it is up to historians to make use of the archives.'

We would have to wait until July 2015 to hear an official statement on the subject, delivered by François Hollande during a press conference in Yaoundé. The French president gave a timid and somewhat muddled response. 'It is true', he admitted, 'that there were extremely difficult, even tragic episodes, as after independence there was repression in the Sanaga-Maritime, in the Bamileke region. And we are, as I have been everywhere, open to the history books being opened, and the archives as well.' However, it took another seven years for this effort to begin to materialise: at the beginning of his second presidential term, President Emmanuel Macron set up a 'memorial commission' intended to 'shed light' on the bloody decolonisation of Cameroon. The initiative was firmly supervised, however, since the heads of this official commission were directly appointed by the Élysée.[17]

In any case, these political initiatives attest to a certain anxiety in Paris. While the regime of Paul Biya, an old 'friend of France', is now in an advanced state of decrepitude, and anti-French feeling gains ground in Cameroon, as in the rest of the French-speaking African countries, French leaders have understood that it was now urgent to come out of denial. History does not belong only to the past: it is still burning.

1

Preludes:
The Unsolvable Colonial Equation

It was in the name of human rights and the defence of oppressed races that Germany was stripped of colonies where, by her own admission, violence and even the extermination of weak peoples had been established as a theory of law. This mass of human beings that Germany had violated was handed over to the trusteeship of other nations, those that the peace treaty, in Article 22, calls the 'developed nations', and to which it entrusts, for the betterment of these races, what it calls the 'sacred mission of civilisation'. It is in application of this article that France's personal mission has been extended to Togo and Cameroon.

— Albert Sarraut,
La Mise en valeur des colonies françaises, 1923

In the wake of 1945, across all colonial theatres from Indonesia to Ghana, from Algeria to Kenya, and from Indochina to Angola, the European powers found themselves in a difficult position. The once-hegemonic metropoles of the Old Continent had been demoted to second-rank players on an international stage now dominated by two superpowers, namely the United States and the Soviet Union. While Washington and Moscow were hostile to keeping the European colonial empires just as they were, London, Paris, Brussels and Lisbon also faced contradictions of their own. For they were now confronted by colonised peoples who could no longer tolerate being

kept in their submissive state in the name of being civilised. Europe's
colonial powers were trying to resolve an equation that in many
regards seemed unsolvable: how could they maintain their hold on
the world, when everything pointed towards the end of these empires,
which in previous decades had been so crucial to their power and
prosperity?

In few places was this problem posed quite so explicitly as it was
in the land today known as Cameroon. Having repeatedly changed
its name, master, capital and borders since the Berlin Conference of
1884–85, in 1945 this territory was not a colony like any other. After
the First World War, it had been placed under League of Nations
supervision and entrusted to French and British administration, in
the form of the so-called mandate system. But this dubious legal
device, which established a kind of 'colonialism with a human face',
soon fell into disuse: as the League of Nations collapsed in the 1930s,
the Levant territories placed under French and British mandates –
today's Iraq, Lebanon, Syria, Palestine and Jordan – in turn gained
their independence.

When the colonial empires in Asia and the Middle East began to
crumble in the late 1940s, French leaders saw their mandates in Africa –
Togo and Cameroon – as dangerous fracture lines. Cameroon,
strategically located in the heart of Central Africa and stirred up by
assertive popular movements in the aftermath of the Second World
War, was the focus of careful attention in Paris. If the gusts of decolonisation blew through this crack, it risked bringing the whole colonial
edifice crashing down. To understand how the situation in Cameroon
escalated, leading the French authorities to wage a murderous war
there in the 1950s, we should firstly look back to its recent history. This
was a particular territory which, while theoretically enjoying a more
liberal legal status than other colonial societies, in practice suffered the
same injustices.

Kamerun, Cameroun, Cameroons: a problem of sovereignty

After the European powers signed the Treaty of Berlin (1885), laying down the rules for the famous 'scramble for Africa', the Germans established themselves on the west coast of the land they called 'Kamerun'. This name was a translation of the word Camarões, which Portuguese explorers had used to name the Wouri estuary, rich in ghost shrimp. Having had the Douala kings sign a steeply unequal protectorate treaty in 1884, the Germans gradually extended their influence into the hinterland, reaching Lake Chad in the north in 1894. The territory was further extended thanks to the Agadir Incident in 1911. This *coup de force* – the Germans sent a gunboat into the Bay of Agadir to pressure the French – allowed Berlin to extend its grip over equatorial Africa in exchange for abandoning its claims to Morocco. Kamerun gained 272,000 square kilometres by incorporating former territories of French Equatorial Africa (AEF).

Conquered by force of arms, its people subjected to forced labour and criss-crossed by a rail network that allowed the extraction of its agricultural, forestry and mining riches, German Kamerun did not survive the First World War. The French, who owned Gabon, Middle-Congo, Chad and Ubangi-Shari, and the British, masters of neighbouring Nigeria, took control of the territory in 1916. This de facto rule was then enshrined by the Treaty of Versailles in 1919 and by the diplomatic negotiations that followed over the subsequent years.

Like the other German and Ottoman dependencies, Kamerun became an international territory under League of Nations supervision. Divided into parts – much like Togoland, which had also been taken from the Germans – it was entrusted to the victors in the form of mandates. France obtained four-fifths of the land area (Cameroun français), while the United Kingdom received the two western parts bordering Nigeria (the British Cameroons). Given the mandate territories' special status, Paris and London were formally accountable to the League of Nations and undertook to report annually to the Permanent Mandates Commission to ensure that they were fulfilling their stipulated responsibilities. These tasks included guaranteeing the 'well-being and development' of the local populations.

Kamerun's new status resulted from two compromises: a French–British deal on its new borders and an agreement between the United States and the European powers as to the legal status of the territorial entities thus created. While London and Paris would readily have *annexed* the dependencies of the defeated powers, they had to come to terms with Washington, which played a decisive role in the Allied forces' victory. It was US president Woodrow Wilson who had pushed for mandates. While this solution was designed as a temporary compromise, it harboured a huge contradiction: it allowed the European powers to extend their colonial influence, even as it weakly called on them to respect the fundamental rights of the peoples under their administration.

Since mandate status did not explicitly recognise the sovereignty of London and Paris over their respective Cameroons, it left open this crucial question: who, exactly, was sovereign in the former German Kamerun? The League of Nations, the mandatory powers – or the inhabitants themselves? The legal mechanism by which the League of Nations delegated their administration to the colonial powers on behalf of the local populations only highlighted the paradoxes, ambiguities and hypocrisies of the entire colonial system. This was, after all, an inherently racist system that nonetheless claimed to be humanist.

The false pretences of a 'humanist colonial order'

While on paper the mandate system placed limits on the French and British authorities, in practice it did not stop them from administering their Cameroons using the same methods they employed in their other African possessions. As in the era of German control, under the pretext of development, a system of forced labour exacted a terrible price on both the colonial plantations and the building sites set up by the French administration. Taxes of all kinds – on homes, tom drums, bicycles, dogs and so on – weighed on populations who had only limited access to the cash economy. The 'natives' were crushed under the most violent racism. Obliged to bend over backwards for the whites, they had to submit to nonsensical classifications that ranked the region's 'races', 'tribes' and 'ethnic groups' – the Bassa, Bamileke, Boulou, Djem, Bene, Pygmies and so on – in an explicit hierarchy.

Of course, a few charitable souls occasionally expressed outrage at the most flagrant excesses. But no one seemed to be moved by the fate reserved for Africans between the wars. In Geneva, French officials shamelessly justified themselves before the Mandates Commission: they explained that lifting the inhabitants to the level of civilisation required certain strains and sacrifices. Wouldn't it be better if the 'natives' cured themselves of their natural laziness and broke out of their age-old savagery? Through the magic of such rhetoric, compulsory labour, iniquitous taxes and brutality were integrated into France's great colonial endeavour on an equal footing with schools, where bodies and minds were disciplined with canes and with the vaccination campaigns of military doctor Eugène Jamot (1879–1937), whose 'exemplary struggle against sleeping sickness' was especially revered.

While the French and British administered and exploited this country much like they did their own colonies, they knew that they were not entirely at home in former Kamerun, which had now become international territory. Ambiguous as a legal device, the mandate system above all encouraged them to step up their propaganda. More than elsewhere, the colonial powers insisted on the humanitarianism of their efforts, highlighted the health and social infrastructure that they were building and swore that they sought nothing more than 'the well-being and development' of the locals, as per the promises made to the League of Nations. In other words, the powers 'supervising' these territories sought to turn the mandates into showcases for a humanist colonial endeavour. This illusion was especially convincing for the League's observers, who not only shared the civilisational ethos of the time but never actually visited the territories concerned and only interviewed the natives presented to them by the mandate powers.

Official double talk was thus taken to unprecedented extremes. Sometimes it was full of contradictions: in a 1931 dossier devoted to the League of Nations, the very official *Togo-Cameroun* review, which ardently defended the French presence in these two territories, took offence at the annexationist ambitions of the British, who stood accused of hoping to integrate part of the Cameroons into their Nigerian colony. 'Sovereignty in a mandated country . . . belongs to the community of inhabitants who live on its soil,' it stridently reminded readers. 'In the Mandates Commission's estimation, the mandatory power is managing a territory that is not its own, and it takes great care to ensure that no practical infringement should undermine this principle.'[1]

Resistance and Insubordination

Never consulted at the Berlin Conference, the Versailles Conference or the Mandates Commission, the populations who were not yet termed Cameroonians nevertheless did not keep their silence. While some, like the Douala chiefs in 1884, temporarily believed that they could do business with the colonisers, others, in greater numbers, opposed them with weapons in hand. For some years, the Germans had to fight dozens of revolts across the country. German officials were steeped in a belligerent racism, and some devised radical 'solutions'. 'The Bamileke, who are constantly fighting and waging war against each other, are an evil and troublesome race,' one official noted in a 1902 report. 'The only solution is to exterminate them all.'[2]

As unrest continued after the First World War, the French pursued the pacification of troublesome regions. They in turn destroyed rebel villages and harshly repressed the insubordinate populations.[3] Yet over time, the colonial war changed in character. The concern was no longer so much the conquest of territory as the subjugation of its inhabitants. Targeted operations against armed rebels gave way to a relentless system of domination, surveillance and control, which would allow the colonisers to extract maximum profit on an ongoing basis. In French Cameroon – where there were some 2,400 Europeans compared to 3 million Africans in the early 1930s – the colonists reigned supreme. They monopolised the most fertile land, occupied the strategic points of the local economy and benefited from the devoted efforts of a particularly zealous administration, gendarmerie and police force. It was their companies who drew all the profits from the exploitation of palm oil, rubber, bananas, cocoa, coffee, tropical timber and precious metals.

The gradual changes brought about by the colonial penetration of this territory – from the conquest of land to the discipline of bodies and the subjugation of souls – turned lifestyles upside down. The natives were placed under the colonial regime's control, given some partial schooling, evangelised and subjected to forced labour that decimated entire regions. They also invented new ways of resisting. Now unable to engage in an open armed rebellion, they found other, more discreet, if not clandestine, ways of escaping colonial control. Subterfuge, small infractions and petty acts of sabotage became common. It was as if they were trying to preserve what was left of their freedom from one day to the next, and to survive the unbearable injustices of the colonial system. Ancestral knowledge, local cults and inherited beliefs, which the whites struggled to understand and summarily dismissed as 'sorcery', served as existential refuges. But the traditions themselves were being reshaped. Sacred lands and forests were profaned by the colonial machine. Social relations and regional balances were undermined by the rise of the cash economy and the conversion to export crops. Family and generational hierarchies were turned upside down. The traditional political order was shattered and challenged from all sides. Serving as auxiliaries, the 'native chiefs' (*chefs indigènes*) were controlled by the French administration, which readily replaced them when their village militias – used to recruit labour and levy taxes on the population – failed to show sufficient 'firmness'.

When all resistance became impossible, the last-resort solution was to flee. Tens of thousands of villagers left their native regions behind and swelled the ranks of the proletariat that was now burgeoning in the urban centres. While far from huge, towns such as Edea, Ebolowa, Dschang, Bafoussam, Nkongsamba and Ngaoundéré became regional hubs attracting new populations. Yaoundé, the administrative capital and seat of the French governor, and Douala, the port city through which flowed everything entering and leaving Cameroon, directly connected this territory to the rest of the world. But urban life was also known to encourage mixing, innovation and the circulation of ideas. The natives who settled in these cities thus also became the focus of vigilant attention by the colonial police forces. Concentrated in destitute neighbourhoods on the outskirts of the 'European city', these urban pariahs were regularly subjected to mass arrests, arbitrary deportations and other disciplinary measures. Described in police reports as 'vagrants', 'anarchic' and 'detribalised', these populations were, after all, sensitive to new ideas – and on the lookout for new opportunities.

In a society that was both divided and on the move, where people feared the common enemy – the white man – without rejecting everything that he had brought with him, new ideas were emerging.

A 'new political and intellectual cartography' gradually took hold in the minds of the native populations.[4] In this context, a form of patriotism and even nationalism was awakened. This was, without doubt, a nationalism of uncertain make-up: Cameroon, with its shifting borders, multiple languages and tangled histories, remained to be invented. This was also a hybrid nationalism, since individual allegiances remained steeped in lines of descent, villages and the 'local soil'. Finally, it was a paradoxical nationalism, since the national mould was itself an imported category. But a national imaginary circulated all the same, as if smuggled in, among the native populations.[5] The interwar generation understood the arbitrary nature of colonial rule all the better because it had been born under German occupation and wondered why it should now consider itself French or British.

1940: 'Vive le Cameroun libre!'

The Great Depression, which hit the colonies hard in the 1930s, and the Second World War, which unleashed nationalist and racist passions in the 1940s, were two crucial stages in African populations' rising political consciousness. They also marked the state administration's growing interference in colonial affairs. Of course, the state had always had some presence in the colonies. But the collapse of global agricultural prices, the strengthening of protectionism around the world, and the rise of various dangers in Europe prompted the colonial administration to become more actively involved. It increasingly operated outside of its strictly regalian role in order to step up production and resolve social conflicts.

Fuelled by the new economic and international conjuncture, there were increasingly recurrent confrontations between the ever-more-vocal natives and the white settlers, whose living standards suffered market fluctuations. The outbreak of hostilities in Europe in 1939 heightened tensions: while the colonists, who benefited greatly from the war economy, were enjoying a return to prosperity, Cameroonians faced quite a different situation. Not only did they see their living standards plummet as a result of inflation, they were also reduced to the roles of manual labourers and cannon fodder. Thousands of Cameroonians, known as 'volunteers', were sent to the front. Many of them died for France on distant battlefields, and close to seven thousand others returned only after long years away – sometimes proud but often stirred to rebellion.

The rift between the Vichy regime and Free France also had an impact on the African colonies, which General de Gaulle, now confined to London, tried to enlist in the fight against the Nazis. While the colonists in Cameroon were far from unanimously hostile to Marshal Pétain, it was in Douala that the Free French commander Philippe Leclerc landed on 27 August 1940. He proclaimed himself colonel and general commissioner of French Cameroon, rallied most of the European colonists and civil servants to his side, and had posters put up announcing that Cameroon – the first 'liberated' territory – had joined France in resistance: 'Cameroon proclaims its political and economic independence. *Vive la France! Vive le Cameroun libre!*' These slogans surely had a striking impact.

One section of the Cameroonian population was especially shaken during this period of war and crisis: the members of the small native elite who served as auxiliaries to the colonial administration. Described as *évolués* (advanced) and sometimes granted French nationality, this segment of the population embodied the paradoxes of colonisation. Born before the First World War, almost always Christian (Catholic or Protestant), and mostly working as junior civil servants (court or post office clerks, secretaries, teachers, writer-interpreters), these young men owed their social rise to France, whose official ideals they often took up as their own. But as they rubbed shoulders on a daily basis with the French – their superiors in the hierarchy – they knew better than anyone the limits of 'colonial humanism'.

Because of this unique position, not all of them responded in the same way when war broke out. Whether for their own tactical reasons or out of conviction, some championed the greatness of Germany and even called for Kamerun's return to a German orbit. Most of these native 'traitors to the nation' were executed at the start of the conflict. Others, in greater numbers, supported France. Such was the case of the militants of the French–Cameroonian Youth (Jeucafra), an organisation set up by the colonial administration in 1938 to counter 'Germanophile' propaganda. Jeucafra played a decisive role in the political socialisation of this generation and the ripening of its national feeling. Its members did not support France as blindly as their rather well-funded slogans might suggest ('Born French, we intend to remain French until we die'). As the war dragged on in Europe, they used their closeness to the French to try to advance the natives' cause, or at least to raise certain popular demands. Trained as administrative intermediaries, they became political mediators, too.[6] This generation of *évolués* also took an interest in colonial and international affairs.

1945: a new world order

In February 1944, the Free French authorities, still headed by a provisional government, organised the Brazzaville conference on the colonies' future. This event illustrated the ambiguities of a colonial system that intended to perpetuate itself while claiming to serve the interests of the colonised populations. General de Gaulle promised much at the conference: trade union freedom for Africans, equal wages, abolition of the *indigénat* status and forced labour, and a representative assembly in each territory. But these promises remained strictly limited: the final declaration of the conference categorically ruled out 'any possibility [for the colonial territories] of evolving outside the French bloc' and 'any constitution for self-government, even as a distant prospect'.

The Free French authorities sought to reassert their hold on their African territories, while promising some concessions to the colonised. Such commitments owed to their recognition that the international balance of power emerging at the end of the Second World War was more unfavourable than ever to the continuation of an unchanged colonial order. European hegemony had already been undermined by the rising US and Soviet presence in global affairs and by the growing role of law in international relations since the end of the First World War, and in 1945 was severely under threat.

However, the colonial powers, with the United Kingdom and France in the lead, managed to salvage the fundamentals. Although the UN Charter foregrounded the 'self-determination of peoples', London and Paris succeeded in limiting the scope of the text signed by fifty independent states in San Francisco on 26 June 1945. Despite its loftier notes, the charter endorsed the continued existence of 'non-self-governing territories'. Still administered by the colonial powers, the League of Nations—mandate territories that had not achieved independence became 'trust territories' of the new UN. With a Trusteeship Council replacing the Mandates Commission, the UN perpetuated the prewar mandate system with barely altered provisions.

In a time when the world was shaken, colonised peoples quite understandably saw the dominant powers' wartime promises as useful tools for demanding an improvement in their situation. Didn't the Atlantic Charter, signed in 1941 by US president Franklin D. Roosevelt and British prime minister Winston Churchill, declare 'the right of all peoples to choose the form of government under which they will live'? And hadn't the Brazzaville conference promised Africans 'the raising of their standard of living'? As for Article 76 of Chapter XII of the UN Charter, devoted to the trusteeship system, had it not called on the administering authorities to 'promote' among the peoples maintained under their trusteeship 'their progressive development towards self-government or independence'? Even if the wording was ambiguous, this text became an important argument for the national movements that were now taking form.

Settlers vs trade unionists

While the relative liberalism that inspired certain international texts encouraged these movements, we should not ignore the influence of other currents of thought which, while less focused on the principles of international law, did foreground the ideal of social justice. As many historians have suggested, the notion of equality, in its everyday, concrete form, played at least as decisive a role in raising the political awareness of the colonised as did relatively abstract ideas of nationhood. As we have seen, Cameroonian national identity in fact long remained uncertain, hybrid and in many ways paradoxical.

Communism – as upheld by the Soviet Union from 1917 and seemingly triumphant in 1945 – hardly had a monopoly among these new currents of thought, but did play a decisive role. Without doubt, Communist thinking, as formulated by European revolutionary parties in the nineteenth and twentieth centuries, took time to put down roots in the colonies. The circulation of such literature was in any case strictly controlled by a particularly conservative administration. But faced with fearsome economic exploitation and fused social and racial inequalities, the thirst for justice among the colonised inspired growing numbers to take an interest in Communism or, at least, to see that it resonated with their concrete situation. As both formal and informal exchanges developed with the rest of the world, the echoes of Marxist thinking, Leninist doctrines and even the anti-imperialist congresses in Baku (1920) and Brussels (1927) reached the colonies. Trade unions – not always Communist-inspired – played an important role in building mobilisations and coordinating African workers in struggle. Throughout Africa, the spirit of revolt among the colonised, which had long been diffuse but stifled, found expression in trade union organisations that were finally open to the natives. Groups of planters, civil servants and ex-servicemen formed to claim their rights. It was these concrete and immediate demands that served as the breeding ground for broader slogans, as the thirst for individual justice met the desire for collective emancipation. Concrete equality, trade unionists explained, was not possible in a subjugated society, subject to the goodwill of a small and foreign caste.

The nascent trade union movement thus became the platform where social demands and national aspirations crossed paths. It also fostered closer ties between European and African activists. Such was the chemistry that developed in Cameroon around the Communist activist Gaston Donnat. Posted to Cameroon in April 1944, this French schoolteacher made contact with progressive European civil servants and African activists, some of whom were active in Jeucafra. Drawing inspiration from similar initiatives in other French colonies in Africa, this small group set up a 'Marxist study circle', which served as a forum for exchange and political education. It was from this group that, at the end of 1944, a few months after the Brazzaville conference, there emerged the United Confederal Trade Unions of Cameroon (USCC), affiliated with France's own General Confederation of Labour (CGT).

The rise of a structured trade union movement obviously worried the European settlers, who profited from an inequality closely identified with the colonial regime itself. The French colonists in Cameroon were particularly reactionary, and from 2 to 8 September 1945 they organised an Estates General on French colonisation in Douala, to which they invited their counterparts from French sub-Saharan Africa. 'One of the fundamental errors of the Brazzaville conference', said the leader of the settlers in French Equatorial Africa, 'was to have tried to jump the gun by denying the species's biological laws for the evolution of races.' The already deep rift between the colonists and the natives was widening. While the former made arrogant and defiant gestures towards a colonial administration they considered overly liberal, the latter took advantage of the 'spirit of Brazzaville' to advance their demands.

A few days after the colonists' Estates General, at the exact moment that Jeucafra was holding a congress in the economic capital Douala, the rivalry turned into a bloody confrontation. At the end of September 1945, taking as a pretext a railway workers' strike in the city, as well as a demonstration with anti-European overtones, the colonists launched a massive retaliatory manhunt. The French colonial administration, overwhelmed by the pace of events, sided with the settlers in revolt, supplying them with weapons and allowing the air force to machine-gun the native crowd. The outcome of this massacre, reminiscent on a smaller scale of the events in Sétif and Guelma in Algeria a few weeks earlier, would never be known (see box below).

The riots in Douala in September 1945

On 20 September 1945, Cameroonian railway workers from Bonabéri, on the outskirts of Douala, went on strike to demand higher pay. Faced with the intransigence of the colonial administration, the strikers and young unemployed workers escaped the control of the recently authorised unions. As the days passed the strike spread to Douala itself. On 24 September, a gathering of several thousand people turned into a riot; shots were reportedly fired, shops were looted and the New Bell prison was surrounded. Some of the colonists retaliated with a real vendetta. 'The European crowd visibly swelled, prey to a violent excitement, the women shouted death threats, the men vociferated that the trade unionists had to be hanged, the Communists shot and the Negroes mercilessly decimated in order to restore order,' wrote the governor's deputy in his memoirs.[7] The French trade unionist Étienne Lalaurie was almost lynched by the settler mob, who went so far as to invade Douala airport to order the plane taking him away to turn back.

Governor Henri Pierre Nicolas then gave in to the colonists, arming them and authorising the air force to use machine guns 'if necessary to clear the ground'.[8] The manhunt began. The most spectacular episode was the machine-gunning of the Cameroon rioters by the air force – while, on the ground, machine guns mounted on lorries completed the operation. 'I had received spoken orders from Captain Valentin to shoot on sight at all natives during curfew hours (7 p.m. to 6 a.m.)', a gendarmerie lieutenant later testified.[9] As one police report put it, around fifteen Cameroonian corpses were fished out of the Wouri: 'All [had been] shot in the back, most often with hunting rifles.'[10] The real outcome of the events of September 1945 is very unclear even today. The official death toll is nine. The governor's deputy would speak of 'around sixty dead', and Pierre Messmer, future French high commissar in Cameroon, of seventy to eighty. The real total is doubtless much higher.

Plugging the gaps in the colonial order

The massacres in Sétif and Guelma, like the ones in Douala, received very little media coverage. They illustrate the insoluble contradictions of a colonial order which, while claiming to be humane and generous, was unable to reconcile its contrasting objectives. The 'advancement' of local populations – a mere pretext for controlling them – did little to conceal the real aims of colonisation: the economic exploitation of subjugated countries and the strategic empowerment of the colonial power in question.

While colonial affairs were of little interest to the European powers' metropolitan populations – who, in the immediate postwar period, were preoccupied with the urgent concerns of reconstruction – they did worry the business world and politicians. But proceeding without a clear roadmap and faced with differing situations in each colony, political leaders made contradictory decisions that further undermined the imperial system. This was particularly true in Asia: while the colonial authorities were forced to negotiate independence in some territories, they hoped to reconquer others by force. These different scenarios – sometimes combined with and punctuated by deadly wars – led to the recognition of the independence of India (1947), Indonesia (1949) and, later, Indochina (1954).

In Africa, too, the colonial powers harshly repressed social and political movements. But, alternately wielding both the stick and the carrot, they also announced reforms in order to 'calm things down'. The result of fragile political compromises, the institutional reforms decided after 1945 were once again based on unstable balances. This was the case in France, where the Constituent Assembly steered the colonial regime in a relatively more liberal direction, more in keeping with the spirit of the times. The Constitution of the Fourth Republic recognised in its preamble that 'France intends to lead the peoples for whom it is responsible to the freedom to administer themselves and to manage their own affairs democratically'. This document, which came into force in October 1946, set up assemblies supposed to represent the colonised populations in Paris and in each of the overseas territories. But these declarations of principle and institutional reforms were simultaneously hollowed out by discriminatory measures: these included the creation of a 'double electoral college' allowing the over-representation of European colonists in these assemblies, the appointment of certain 'representatives' by the administration, the drastic restriction of the African electorate, and the draconian preselection of candidates.

The contradictions of the colonial system were even more glaring in territories such as Cameroon, which remained under international trusteeship. Taking advantage of the vagueness surrounding the provisions of the UN Charter, the ruling powers managed to turn them to their advantage. Signed in New York in December 1946, the trusteeship agreements – which set out the practical arrangements for administering these territories – allowed the trustee authorities to manage the former mandates 'as an integral part' of their territorial holdings and refrained from setting any deadline for their autonomy or independence. Here again, provisions that were supposed to be liberal backfired on the populations they were meant to serve: the trust territories would be administered as if they were mere colonies, and for an indefinite period at that.

In the months following the end of the Second World War, the colonial powers managed to plug the gaps in Africa that threatened the foundations of their empires. Making skilful use of an 'evolutionist' rhetoric – which reassured public opinion and allies abroad, who were also convinced that African peoples were inferior – the colonial powers promised gradually to shepherd the colonised towards autonomy. As proof of their goodwill, they put the spotlight on the indigenous elites: and indeed, some of these hand-picked figures enjoyed relative material affluence and rose to positions of responsibility, for instance in what were called representative assemblies. These évolués served as tokens of the humanist qualities of a system that remained structurally racist and as a bulwark against the growing demands of the colonised peoples. By encouraging the upward social mobility of a handful of 'elected' individuals chosen for their docility and at the same time limiting access to privileged positions, the timid reformism promoted by the colonial authorities sent a two-sided message to the colonised populations. They were, in effect, told that there could be no freedom without discipline. While this appealed to a small part of the population hankering after individual advancement, such blackmail did little to convince those who, daily forced to endure the colonial order, wanted to hurry along the moment of freedom.

The ideology of development had been present in the League of Nations Covenant sealed in 1922 and became a central theme of imperial discourse after 1945. This expressed a modernisation of the colonial authorities' previous evolutionist and disciplinary discourse. While counting themselves in the camp of 'developed' nations, the Western powers reduced the dominated territories to their alleged condition of 'underdevelopment'; this, in turn, was taken as justification for the colonial investment policy which was supposed to help these populations to catch up. This led to France's creation of the Investment Fund for Economic and Social Development (FIDES) in 1946. In the name of laudable social pretexts, this mechanism enabled France to build up the infrastructure in its colonies – by which they meant primarily ports, roads and railways – that would favour the economic prosperity of metropolitan France, while consolidating its links with its overseas dependencies. Unsurprisingly, the trustee territories, which were less firmly attached to France than the other colonies, received generous loans. Cameroon, the first beneficiary of FIDES, received 36.5 million francs between 1947 and 1953 – 85 per cent of which was allocated to infrastructure and only 10 per cent to 'social amenities'.

The ideological, legal and socio-economic mechanisms introduced after 1945 perpetuated the colonial system, even as that system had to confront its contradictions more than ever before. While the rhetoric was more liberal, this concealed a colonial machine that was just as despotic as it had always been. Behind the promises of future independence, the next phase of colonisation was setting in motion. In the calculations of those in Paris, London and elsewhere who were seeking to solve the insoluble colonial equation, a new form of colonialism was already in the making. It was based on offering limited autonomy to a docile elite, precisely in order to prevent the colonised peoples from laying claim to genuine independence and social justice.

2

The Confrontation Takes Shape (1948–54)

The magic word of independence has now been let loose. If we're not careful, in Africa as elsewhere France will end up being caught unawares.

— Louis-Paul Aujoulat, speech to the National Assembly, June 1954

The twelve men who met at the Chez Sierra bar in Douala on 10 April 1948 surely had no idea quite how important their actions would prove. Yet in the years and decades to come, their country's political life would centre around the political movement they founded that day – the Union of the Populations of Cameroon (UPC).

There was nothing particularly radical about the UPC's initial agenda. Its aim was to 'bring together and organise the inhabitants' of Cameroon, as stated in the movement's articles of association filed with Douala city hall on 12 April 1948. In the end, the UPC's demands went no further than what the French leaders had themselves been promising in previous months. Echoing the Brazzaville Declaration, the UPC called for the 'more rapid development of [Cameroon's] populations and the raising of their living standards'. It also reminded the French and British authorities of the commitments that they had made at the UN, as the manifesto emphasised that the UPC was working 'for greater autonomy for our territory every day'.

The rise of the UPC: making the people sovereign

The colonial administration, which kept a close eye on the *indigène* populations' political and trade union activities, soon recognised what was going on. It immediately understood that this new movement – led by young Cameroonians who had cut their teeth in the Jeucafra, the Marxist study circles and the USCC trade unions – would not stop at trite formulas. The UPC was outwardly taking the colonialists at their word to expose how they promised reforms and then used devious means to neuter them. The UPC highlighted the contradictions of colonialism, which claimed to serve the colonised people but in fact benefited a handful of colonists. The UPC was exploiting the 'breach' that had been opened up by the system of UN supervision. The French administrators thus recognised it as a spanner in the works of the colonial machine.

Colonial circles were right to be concerned. In a moment in the late 1940s when several countries in Asia and the Middle East were gaining independence, social movements and political demands were also on the rise in Africa: these included a general strike in Dakar (at the end of 1945), a miners' strike in South Africa (1946), a peasant uprising in Madagascar (1947), a railway workers' strike in French West Africa (1947–48), mass protests and urban riots in the Gold Coast (1948) and so on. Faced with such widespread unrest, the colonial authorities hesitated. Wavering between the carrot and the stick, they unwittingly showed that the demands of the colonised were justified, while also – paradoxically enough – offering a legal platform for their expression.

It was against this backdrop that the new political groupings of the postwar period emerged. In French-ruled Africa, the Rassemblement démocratique africain (RDA), founded in Bamako in October 1946 and chaired by Félix Houphouët-Boigny (1905–93), then a member of the French National Assembly for Côte d'Ivoire, played a pivotal role in the African political scene. Until the late 1940s connected to the French Communist Party, the RDA was the meeting-place and coordinating body for progressive movements in francophone Africa, most of which were local sections of this party which spanned the different French-ruled territories. This was the case for the Côte d'Ivoire Democratic Party (PDCI), founded by Houphouët in April 1946, as well as all the parties formed in the wake of the Bamako Congress: the Senegalese Democratic Union (UDS), the Niger Progress Party (PPN), the Guinea Democratic Party (PDG) and so on. The UPC, the Cameroonian section of the RDA, belonged to this pan-African universe.

The UPC's affiliation to the RDA was not, however, the thing that most worried the French administration in Cameroon. It soon found a way of surmounting the danger represented by the RDA, as we shall see later on. What alarmed the colonial administrators rather more was the intellectual revolution that the UPC was beginning to foster, drawing on a handful of slogans that were both practical and radical. As the movement rapidly took shape, stepping up its contacts abroad and gaining a hearing among the Cameroonian population, the colonial authorities gradually decided to wage war against it. At first, this was a low-intensity war. But in the mid-1950s, it grew in scale.

We could hardly do justice to the UPC without a brief sketch of its emblematic general secretary, Ruben Um Nyobè. While he was not present at the founding meeting at Chez Sierra, he was the UPC's architect and main driving force from 1948 up until his assassination in 1958. He was born in 1913 in what was known as the Bassa country, at a time when Kamerun was German-ruled. An eyewitness to forced labour and the abuses committed by the French in the interwar years, Um Nyobè belonged to that small class of native civil servants who, educated in the Christian schools, rose through the ranks of the French administration in the 1930s and 1940s. A court clerk, he joined

Jeucafra in 1939, took part in Gaston Donnat's Marxist study circles, and became general secretary of the USCC at the end of 1947. On the strength of these personal, professional and activist experiences, Um Nyobè was convinced that the fight against colonialism was a concrete struggle that was fought in the daily lives of the colonised. The UPC thus saw itself first and foremost as an organisation that stood up for the populations of Cameroon, spanning their different social origins, regional attachments or religious obediences. In the fight against colonial injustices – poverty wages, exorbitant taxes, racial segregation, continual vexations, the various kinds of ill treatment and so on – the UPC was especially counting on the efforts of the trade union movement, from which most of its leaders hailed. But it also made contact with all groups throughout the country that it considered likely to carry its message and inform it about what the administration was up to.

Building ties with traditional associations, farmers' societies, village communities, religious groups, students sent to mainland France, ex-servicemen's organisations and sports clubs, the UPC sought to be both the educator and the spokesman of Cameroon's populations. Um Nyobè and his comrades summoned up boundless energy, distributing an impressive number of pamphlets and newspapers (*La Voix du Cameroun*, *Étoile*, *Lumière*, *Vérité* and so on) and organising rallies, meetings and discussions across the country. Within just a few years, they had established their movement among the most varied social circles.

Having begun with just a hundred members in 1948, the movement claimed seven thousand members the following year and double that number in 1950. Five years later, the head of the French police in Cameroon, Pierre Divol, spoke of a twenty-thousand-member-strong organisation thanks to whom, he claimed, the UPC held 'sway over around 80,000 people'.[1] The neatly structured UPC set up hundreds of base committees throughout the country: in the towns, starting with the main cities Douala and Yaoundé, but also in the villages, in Sanaga-Maritime, in the Bamileke region, in Mungo. Even the north of the country, at first wary of its message, saw the UPC's influence grow: the French police counted three hundred active militants there in 1955. This was undoubtedly the UPC's most spectacular success. By bringing together people of different languages, cultures, religions and classes, who did not always see themselves as having common interests, this organisation helped to politicise a large section of the Cameroonian population in just a few years. 'Everything is political and everything must be given a political framing,' explained Um Nyobè.[2] 'Religion has become political. Business is political. Even sport is political. Politics concerns everything and everything concerns politics. To say that you are not interested in politics is to admit that you have no desire for life.'

The logic of colonialism cast the colonised as mere tools, mostly valuable as hands and muscles (as labourers, soldiers and so on). In contrast to this, the UPCists – as they came to be known – used concrete, everyday language to call on their compatriots to break with the slave morality that colonisation sought to impose. Cameroonians, the UPC insisted, were individually and collectively sovereign and masters of their own fate. Recognising this was both the first stage of decolonisation and its essential goal.

In fact, as many researchers have pointed out, the politicisation that can be observed in Cameroon during this period, and Cameroonians' massive support for the UPC's ideals, did not owe to the appeal of nationalist slogans alone. More subtly, they reflected a vast movement of individual and collective emancipation, which combined different personal, social, local and generational dimensions. In a bid to represent this diversity of aspirations, the UPC established links with local associations and traditional organisations, such as the Ngondo in Douala and the Kumzse in the Bamileke region, and set up a women's group, the Democratic Union of Cameroonian Women

(UDEFEC), in 1952, and a youth wing, the Cameroon Democratic Youth (JDC), in 1954.

Striking in terms of both the UPC's discourse and its actions is this organisation's unique blend of pragmatism and determination. Equally remarkable was the radical method used by Ruben Um Nyobè to advance his ideas. No doubt because he had been a court clerk, but also for strategic reasons, the UPC general secretary, who was a reader of Gandhi, would throughout his life retain a distinct attachment to legality and a fundamental opposition to the use of violence. The Cameroonians' efforts, he felt, were aimed above all at forcing the powers who administered the country to respect their own national laws and the international texts which they had underwritten. In other words, the French and the British must be made to face up to their own contradictions. Weapons would be no use in this regard.

Completing this line of reasoning, the UPC general secretary was always careful to distinguish colonialism, which he abhorred, from the peoples of Europe. 'We do not confuse the people of France with French colonialists,' he repeated, to hammer home the contradiction between the colonial authorities' actions and the principles to which they laid claim. Um Nyobè frequently paid tribute to the French Resistance against Nazism, emphasising that 'the people of France have always been and remain the symbol of progress and democracy. The only people who are anti-French are those who, in the name of France, pursue a reactionary policy contrary to the republican principles that inspire the people of France.'[3] In this respect, it is interesting that UPC activists sometimes sang 'La Marseillaise' at their rallies – as the French police reports noted, with a certain bafflement. The UPC did adopt its own songs, its own symbols and its own flag – a black crab on a red background – to represent its intended break with the colonial order. But its members also liked to remind their opponents which people in Cameroon could really be called the *enfants de la patrie* raising their banner *contre la tyrannie*.

Reunification and independence: overthrowing the colonial order

Cameroon's special legal status also does much to explain the UPC's specific features. Precisely because this territory, as Um Nyobè put it, 'benefited from the international trusteeship regime', Cameroonian patriots could – and, as far as the UPC general secretary was concerned, should – wage a legalistic and peaceful struggle. Far from being forced into a head-on confrontation with the metropole, as most colonised peoples were, Cameroonians could not only exploit the contradictions between the French and the British, but also bypass both of them by appealing to the UN directly.

This was a crucial feature of the UPC's political strategy: its reliance on the UN to force the French and British authorities into a compromise. To get around the farce of the visiting missions that the United Nations sent to Cameroon at three-year intervals (1949, 1952, 1955), the UPC, through its supporters, sent tens of thousands of petitions to the UN headquarters in New York. Much to the dismay of the French authorities, in the 1950s the UPC won the right to have its representatives heard by the UN Trusteeship Council. Um Nyobè thus got three hearings at the UN headquarters between 1952 and 1954. It was there that he explained his vision of a reunited and independent Cameroon with the greatest finesse.

Rarely debated since the partition of German Kamerun just after the First World War, the question of the unity of Cameroon resurfaced at the end of the 1940s. For the members of the UPC, who included the issue in their manifesto from 1948 onwards and gradually forged closer links with anticolonial circles in the British zone, the unity of Cameroon was both an end goal and a means of action. The insistence that Cameroon was 'one and indivisible' helped to counter the annexationist ambitions of the French, who were desperate to integrate their Cameroon into the French Union, and those of the British, who saw their Cameroons as mere dependencies of neighbouring Nigeria.

During this period, the British and the French adopted different attitudes to the broad movement towards decolonisation: London was, in general, more liberal in its approach. Promoting the reunification of Cameroon enabled the UPC not only to play on rivalries between Paris and London – which were particularly intense, despite the muffled language of bilateral diplomacy – but also to use the favourable developments they saw elsewhere in the British Empire as leverage to pressure the French. If British Cameroon won its freedom from London rule, in accordance with the goals set out in the 1946 trusteeship agreements, what would happen to French Cameroon? Raising the issue of reunification thus allowed the UPC to pose the question of Cameroon's sovereignty and to remind French authorities that they, too, had signed up to agreements which called for peoples in trustee territories to gain 'self-government or independence'.

Independence was indeed the UPC's central aim. At first, however, those who were just beginning to call themselves nationalists were rather coy about this delicate issue. Aware that Cameroon was still greatly unprepared, they initially settled for demanding that a deadline be set for eventual independence. It was only later – realising that the colonial authorities were deliberately maintaining this state of unpreparedness in order to keep trusteeship going indefinitely – that the UPC stepped up their tone. Having at first unsuccessfully demanded that a deadline be set, they themselves proposed the date of 1956 (ten years after the signing of the trusteeship agreements).

The question of independence deserves particular attention. As the American historian Frederick Cooper points out – and contrary to what might now be readily imagined – this issue was not the priority for the African political parties that emerged in the aftermath of the Second World War. For the UPC, like other such movements, the most urgent concern was to improve the material lot of the colonised people and to ensure that they enjoyed the same rights as citizens in the metropole. 'In the early 1950s,' Cooper notes, 'the Senghors and the Houphouët-Boignys tried to turn French citizenship into something meaningful and useful to their constituents, rather than to claim another sort of sovereignty.'[4] In other words, the demand for equality came first.

Compared to most similar organisations in French Africa, the UPC placed a distinctive stress on the texts issued by the UN, which, in 1946, had offered autonomy or independence to territories under trusteeship. 'Since we are denied equality, we demand freedom,' was the gist of their position. It made this switch well before the other progressive parties in French-ruled Africa, most of which did not formally take up the cause of independence until the end of the 1950s, sometimes even after decision-makers in Paris had settled on this course of action.

In this regard it is interesting to mention Léopold Sédar Senghor's visit to Cameroon in September 1953. Giving a talk in Douala, the Senegalese MP expressed the view that independence was a pipe dream, given that different nations were increasingly interdependent. For this, he was taken to task by the UPC's vice-president Ernest Ouandié, who was in the audience. Looking down on his interlocutor, Senghor claimed that it would take another twenty years for France's African colonies to achieve even a basic domestic autonomy.

Counter-fire: France's covert war against the UPC

The UPC's growing success soon became a headache for the French authorities. How could they fight a political movement which, even while opposing France head-on, scrupulously respected legality and the tools provided by international law? Up till 1955, it found no comprehensive answer to this question. The colonial authorities in Yaoundé and in the various administrative regions of Cameroon initially settled for using a vast array of stratagems to make the UPC buckle or to discredit its leaders.

As in any authoritarian regime – and a colony is such a regime, by definition – the French administration relied on police surveillance to combat its opponents. The UPC leader's slightest movements were spied on and their correspondence opened and read; every UPC meeting was the subject of a detailed report, drawn up by either a civil servant or an undercover agent. When we leaf through the archives we are surprised by the welter of details that the intelligence reports provide about the Cameroonian nationalists.

Armed with this knowledge of nationalist circles, the French authorities engaged in constant harassment of UPC leaders. This covert war was rarely spectacular, but it was particularly damaging for poorly resourced activists who needed the greatest inventiveness just to find premises, print leaflets or organise rallies. The UPC's headquarters were raided on the thinnest of pretexts, and its activists often had their archives, equipment and money seized without any hope of recourse. Protests were regularly banned on the grounds that they would represent a 'disturbance to public order', and UPC activists were arrested every time they tried to organise any kind of event.

UPC officials in public-sector jobs, such as the doctor Félix Moumié, who became the organisation's president in 1952, or Ernest Ouandié, a teacher, were frequently transferred from one region to another by authorities keen to disrupt the nationalist movement. Posted to Maroua, in northern Cameroon, in the early 1950s, Moumié was subjected to what French intelligence boss Guy Georgy (1918–2003) proudly called psychological guerrilla warfare. In his memoirs, Georgy amusedly recalls the 'intimidation' tactics he used against the UPC leader, often organising gendarmerie manoeuvres in front of his house in order to make him paranoid.[5]

As for Um Nyobè, who had taken leave from his job in the administration to devote himself to UPC activism, he was targeted by a judicial machine that followed the orders of the political authorities. This machine was especially set in motion in the weeks following his first hearing at the UN in December 1952. In a moment when he was holding rallies across Cameroonian territory, Um Nyobè was taken to task by a particularly zealous administrator, Bernard de Gélis, whose superior had instructed him: 'The success that [Um Nyobè] has just achieved in Douala, Edea and Eseka could encourage him to be bolder . . . When he comes to you he has to stumble and be ridiculed by his potential listeners.'[6]

In the effort to discredit nationalist leaders, colonial rhetoric drew deep from an ideological and even civilisational register. The French press routinely described the UPC as a Communist party following orders from Moscow, even though intelligence reports showed that this was totally untrue. UPC leaders did maintain relations with progressive circles in Europe and sometimes accepted invitations from the 'people's democracies' (Ouandié, for example, attended the World Federation of Democratic Youth council held in Beijing in August 1954). But the confidential report drawn up by the head of the French police in Cameroon in 1955 was blunt: 'The UPC has never been an African Communist party.'[7] Um Nyobè explained in 1953 that 'the colonial peoples can pursue neither the politics of a party, nor that of a state, nor even more so that of a man. Colonial peoples pursue their own politics, the politics of liberation from the colonial yoke.'[8]

These were the years of the Cold War, and the accusation of Communism was mostly a propaganda weapon, aimed at discrediting the UPC in the eyes of both local populations and international bodies. The highly influential Louis-Paul Aujoulat (1910–73), a devout Catholic, had a particular zeal for this anti-Communist rhetoric. Having moved to Cameroon in the 1930s, and been a member of parliament for the territory from 1945 to 1956, he was secretary of state for overseas France in eight cabinets between 1949 and 1953, before becoming minister for health and then labour. For Aujoulat, the fight against the UPC was an existential struggle, pitting not only the free world against Communism but also civilisation against a kind of infantile and ungrateful savagery. Um Nyobè and his comrades were, Aujoulat said, no more than 'a clutch of failures and malcontents'.[9]

The same discourse can be found in the preaching of many churchmen from this period. The Catholic hierarchy here was especially reactionary: the apostolic delegate for French-speaking black Africa from 1948 to 1959, appointed by Pope Pius XII, was none other than the fundamentalist archbishop Marcel Lefebvre (1905–91). In Cameroon, his representative from 1935 onwards was Monseigneur René Graffin (1899–1967), who headed a church where blacks were relegated to subordinate positions. Graffin tore up trade unionists' membership cards, condemned public schools and players of the balafon (a traditional African musical instrument, deemed 'pagan') and excommunicated nationalists, whom he readily identified with the godless USSR. Not uncommonly, the secrets revealed by the faithful in the confession booth soon found their way into police reports.

Sham politics: creating an 'African opposition' to the UPC

Systematic opposition to the UPC gradually became an obsession for French officials, who sought to isolate the nationalists from the rest of the population and thus stem the spread of the protest 'virus'. To this end, the authorities drew up appalling lists in which every Cameroonian political, trade-union or religious leader was pigeonholed as 'good', 'quite good', 'Francophile' or 'very Francophile' or else as 'doubtful', 'anti-French', 'mediocre', 'unreliable' or 'pro-independence'.[10] These lists dictated the strategy that was meant to be adopted. The most docile Cameroonians were urged to publicly contradict the UPC, or even to physically confront them. The recalcitrant would be encouraged to fall into line and would receive generous financial rewards for doing so. As for those deemed a 'lost cause', they would continue to suffer the authorities' wrath without let-up.

Corruption and intimidation allowed the administration to turn a few fickle UPC members and, above all, to fuel the emergence of a host of Cameroonian political parties favourable to French interests: Cameroonian Social Progress (ESOCAM), the Cameroonian People's Assembly (RPC), the Cameroonian Independents' Coordination (INDECAM) and so on. Conscious that this veneer of autonomy would produce better results, the French authorities kept alive – or even created from scratch – what one administrator called an 'African opposition' to the UPC.

The peculiar thing about this opposition, whose sole aim was to counter the UPC, was that it took up the demands of its adversaries, in distorted fashion, as they gained headway in Cameroonian society. We can thus see what might be called a sham form of politics in which nationalist slogans were gradually turned against their proponents. For instance, Article 1 of the statutes of ESOCAM, founded in June 1949, repeats word for word the UPC's own founding promise ('To bring together and organise the inhabitants of the Territory with a view to fostering the more rapid development of its populations and the raising of their living standards'). Only with Article 2 did it diverge: here the concern was to 'combat all communist ideas' and to work in a 'spirit of loyal collaboration with the representatives of the administering authorities'.[11]

Even more revealing is the evolution of the party founded by Aujoulat in 1951, the Cameroonian Democratic Bloc (BDC, a sort of twin to Senghor's Senegalese Democratic Bloc). Spearheading the anti-Communist struggle, the BDC ended up adopting some of the UPC's slogans as its own. But, once again, it emptied them of their content. Claiming in 1955 to be a 'realistic Cameroonian nationalism' opposed to the UPC's alleged demand for 'independence in mediocrity', Aujoulat's party explained: '[Nationalism] is not only permissible, it is healthy. It leads us to wish not for this independence – a deception, because it risks being hollow -- but for a more secure independence: autonomy.'[12]

As if by magic, these pro-French parties – for the most part empty shells which rarely recruited beyond their original ethnic circles – won all the elections held. They thus prevented the much more popular UPC candidates from entering the Territorial Assembly of Cameroon (ATCAM). Electoral fraud, an old colonial habit, was surely running at full tilt in Cameroon. Like his colleagues, Guy Georgy, the man who harassed Félix Moumié in the north of the country, helped out so-called administrative candidates. It was Georgy, as he recalled in his memoirs, who launched the political career of Ahmadou Ahidjo, then a humble twenty-three-year-old working for the postal service, by getting him elected to the Territorial Assembly in 1947. 'We practically made people vote for him, by putting packets of voting slips in the ballot boxes,' he reminisced.[13] But it was all in a good cause. Notwithstanding his Francophilia, in May 1960 Ahidjo became the first president of the Republic of Cameroon (see Chapter Five).

For the French authorities, who were essentially guided by the Fourth Republic's own economic and geopolitical interests (see box below), the co-opted elites also served as pawns and as anti-UPC firewalls in dealings with international bodies. On every UN 'visiting mission' to Cameroon, it was they who, as 'the people's elected representatives', were chosen to talk to the international inspectors. While nationalist demonstrators were carefully kept out of the way in the adjacent streets (that is, when they were not being brutally beaten), Francophile elected officials regaled their visitors with talk of Cameroonians' satisfaction at the fate chosen for them by the colonial administration. These were the same people who, sent to New York on the administration's budget, answered Um Nyobè every time he was heard by the UN Trusteeship Council.

France's economic and geopolitical interests in Cameroon in the 1950s

Why did France cling on to Cameroon so tightly in the 1950s? At the time, France had major economic, military and strategic interests in that country. In economic terms, the few thousand colonists controlled all the levers of 'useful Cameroon', between the Bamileke region and Yaoundé, via Douala and the coast: this spanned the most fertile land, allowing for the exploitation of palm oil, rubber, bananas, cocoa, coffee, tropical wood and precious metals. Thanks to forced labour, which was officially authorised until 1946 but continued even after that, the holders of the largest concessions benefited from a cheap workforce and guaranteed outlets in mainland France. This attraction became all the greater a few years before independence, when promising uranium and oil deposits were discovered in the Wouri estuary. French interests primarily meant the interests of certain large private companies, such as the Agriculture and Forestry Company (SAFA), which operated the Dizangue rubber plantation; the French Textiles Development Company (CFDT), which grew cotton in North Cameroon; and Alucam, which produced alumina oxide from hydroelectricity (negotiated at a very advantageous price) from the Edea power station. As well as its natural wealth, Cameroon's economic attractiveness was linked to the port of Douala, Central Africa's commercial crossroads. 'It should not be forgotten that France's position in Cameroon is crucial for its position throughout Central Africa,' emphasised a December 1950 report by the French Overseas Ministry's Department of Economic Affairs and Planning. 'It is certain that whoever holds Douala and Cameroon economically holds Oubangui-Chari [now the Central African Republic] and Chad.'[14]

France's interests were also military and geostrategic in nature. Ever since General de Gaulle and Colonel Leclerc reconquered French colonial Africa – starting from Chad and Cameroon, before their triumphal march back to metropolitan France – these African territories had been seen as a strategic fallback base in the event of trouble in Europe, and even a nuclear attack. After the Second World War, it was mainly thanks to its empire that France was still considered a great power. With the loss of Indochina, followed by the insurrection in Algeria, France's control over a dozen countries in sub-Saharan Africa was the last major card in its hands. The liberation of Cameroon, as of any of these territories, would be likely to inspire other peoples to break free. This domino effect did indeed play out, with the wave of countries granted independence over just a few months in 1960.

Autonomy for the elite or independence for the people? The trap of the Defferre enabling law

France's policy in Cameroon bore some similarities to that which it pursued throughout the French Union more generally. Everywhere, Paris used the carrot and the stick. It sought both to bring oppositionists into line and to recruit Africans who, while giving the impression of defending the interests of the colonised, were in fact playing a part written for them by the colonial power.

Such was the logic behind the events surrounding Félix Houphouët-Boigny at the turn of the 1950s. Considered a Communist at the end of the previous decade and, as a member of the French National Assembly, drafter of a major law banning forced labour, the Ivorian leader was soon forced to make a choice. While his supporters were being severely repressed in Côte d'Ivoire in 1949 and 1950, he was approached by the French government, which was looking to make an ally of the RDA president.

The Ivorian leader accepted the deal. On 18 October 1950, he made official the RDA's separation from the French Communist Party (PCF), signed a political pact with then minister for overseas France François Mitterrand (1916–96), and thus embarked on a brilliant political career.[15] Revisiting this episode four years later, a French military report described the RDA president's highly personal attitude as follows: '[Houphouët] played his game alone, with a great deal of flexibility, hemming and hawing, and cunning worthy of Machiavelli. He took care not to convene either the coordination committee or the party congress.' The latter might have baulked at the idea of 'this about-turn to gradually become a pro-administration party'.[16]

President of the Ivorian Assembly from 1953 to 1959 and a French minister without interruption from 1956 to 1961, in the mid-1950s Houphouët became the most accomplished champion of French-African friendship. He set out this philosophy at the RDA congress held in Conakry in July 1955:

Our fervent wish is that all of France's spiritual families understand that the African Democratic Assembly is turned towards the French people as a whole, desiring to build with them a lasting community whose inevitable family quarrels will not undermine our loyalty, trust or the desire to live together. Who can doubt that the Françafrique experiment is the best hope for the French Union? I don't think anyone can.[17]

Although the UPC claimed allegiance to the RDA until its formal expulsion, which was decided at this same Conakry congress, it was one of this African movement's few local sections to reject the strategic retreat instigated by Houphouët-Boigny. This divergence revealed a fundamental disagreement over two issues: independence and the place of the people. Whereas the UPC called for a total independence that would benefit all of Africa's populations (and in its case, the populations of Cameroon), Houphouët promoted a simple autonomy, within the framework of a 'lasting community' binding France and Africa (Françafrique). This would allow African elites a degree of political power, shared with the French, on behalf of African populations whose demands – as Mitterrand put it – must not be 'political' but strictly 'human, social and economic'.

This limited autonomy was Paris's own favoured option in the mid-1950s. Conscious of the need to make concessions in order to avoid losing everything, French officials began to think about a major reform that would enable them to entrust the handling of the colonial territories' day-to-day affairs to a few hand-picked African elites. This was the aim of the enabling law drafted by the Ministry of Overseas France starting in 1955. Passed by the National Assembly in June 1956 in a moment when Gaston Defferre (1910–86) headed this ministry, this 'Defferre enabling law' established universal suffrage in the colonies, abolished the double-electoral-college system, transformed the territorial assemblies into legislative bodies and created local executives. Made up of African officials, these executives would enjoy certain prerogatives, though they were to be shared with the French administration.

The reform clearly had a tactical dimension, which Mitterrand summed up quite clearly in 1957 when he spoke of a controlled and gradual 'Africanisation' of positions of responsibility. In his book *Présence française et abandon*, he wrote,

> By proceeding in this way, we would undoubtedly succeed in isolating and reducing the ideologically irredeemable hard core, whose presence made any attempt at conciliation futile. On the other hand, the genuine messengers of African liberation would be spared, and the resolve and loyalty of their people and the friendship of France would lead them to the highest destinies.[18]

Beyond their tactical bent the reforms also responded to a both strategic and economic concern. They were strategic because the French leaders, who knew that they could not indefinitely contain the demands of the colonised people, were also watching closely what was happening in the British colonies. They were particularly interested in political developments in the Gold Coast, which was gradually moving towards internal autonomy and then independence (achieved in March 1957). Events in the Gold Coast (later Ghana), nestled in the middle of West Africa, would also have some effect on the French-ruled territories of AOF and even more so on the trustee territory of Togo, which like Cameroon was divided into British and French zones. The French were well aware that the Gold Coast's promised independence was bound to pose the question of British Togo's future and could produce a domino effect.

The reform of the colonial institutions also had an economic dimension. In a moment when development policies and colonial wars (in Indochina and Algeria) were straining the state's finances, there were growing calls to cut spending on the colonies. This stance came to be known as Cartierism after the 1956 publication of a series of articles by *Paris Match* journalist Raymond Cartier in favour of dialling down France's colonial presence (see Chapter Four). This was quite the change when we consider that just three years earlier the same journalist had said of Cameroon: 'We will stay, even if we have to fight for it.' In any case, such economic concerns were not unrelated to the desire to reduce the wage bill of colonial civil servants by transferring certain powers to local elites. They would now be responsible for managing their respective territories' budgets for themselves.

'Crush Communist activities to defend civilisation'

All this marked a shift in the French colonial strategy. It amounted to playing the card of autonomy in order to better undermine demands for independence and promoting docile elites in order to better manage the African masses whose demands continued to be described as irrational and unrealistic. This strategic shift did not escape the Cameroonian nationalists' attention. The journal *Kaso*, published in metropolitan France by Cameroonian students close to the UPC, showed that nationalists were perfectly aware of the real French agenda. 'Without wishing to quibble about words', *Kaso* said in its March 1955 issue, 'we believe that the tunic of "autonomy" is camouflage for an ulterior motive of domination and monetary gain, and is just as fatal to us as Deianira's [poison-soaked tunic] was to Hercules.'

For observers of Cameroon's political and social scene, in 1954–55 there was clearly mounting tension between the nationalists and the colonial administration. The French were worried about the UPC's growing audacity and success. In March 1955, police officer Pierre Divol wrote a sixty-five-page report on the roots that the nationalist movement had developed across the country. In the final sections, he wrote, 'The UPC's influence is undeniable. It has undeniably grown over the last year. And it will continue to grow. But how much so? First, we need to answer another question: knowing the origins, aims, and structure of the UPC and what a presence it has on the ground, what can we put up against it?'[19] In its confidential reports, the French army was no more optimistic. In 1955, it emphasised the UPC's 'great activity', its 'very rapid progress' and its 'ever greater effectiveness'. It was worried to see 'certain districts of Douala (New Bell), Yaoundé (Mokolo, Mvog Mbi) and almost all of the Mungo and Sanaga-Maritime regions [becoming] real nationalist strongholds where the administration's activity [was] systematically frustrated, with the UPC even taking the place of administrative officials'.[20]

In 1948 colonial officials had regarded the UPC as a mere thorn in France's side. But by the mid-1950s they feared that it was an infestation, which could not only take hold in Cameroon but also spread to other colonies. Hence the exasperation of colonial administrators at all levels of the hierarchy. 'It would be a good idea to line up a ban on the

UPC party as soon as possible,' demanded the administrator of Bafang (West) in November 1954. In March 1955, the head of the Eseka sub-division insisted that 'we must be on the trail of all subversive activity in whatever form it takes, without hatred or weakness, hunt down the UPC, ban it and strike at its intractable leaders'. This was necessary, he added, because 'democratic means of fighting the UPC are doomed to failure'.[21] While the French Overseas Ministry was studying legal avenues for banning the UPC, Paris appointed Roland Pré (1907–80), a hardliner, as high commissioner in Yaoundé. He set out his agenda the moment he set foot on Cameroonian soil, in December 1954: 'crush Communist activities' to defend what he called 'civilisation'.

3

'A Smaller Version of Algeria' (1955–58)

The war in Indochina has been lost; another theatre of operations has opened up in North Africa, and others will soon open up in the French Union.
— Lieutenant-Colonel Roger Trinquier, 9 June 1955

Once again, Indochina has an important lesson: for having underestimated our adversaries' strengths and overestimated our own, we headed toward a definitive failure. Our job is not to repeat a similar mistake in Cameroon.
— Lieutenant-Colonel André Trancart (head of the Overseas French coordination section), 11 October 1955

'There are two ways of doing battle: using the law and using force. Typically, humans use laws and animals force. But since playing by the law often proves inadequate, it makes sense to resort to force as well.'[1] These well-known lines from Machiavelli are remarkably applicable to the Cameroon of the 1950s. Through the Defferre enabling law, the French authorities were preparing a partial reform of colonial governance and an 'Africanisation' of some positions of responsibility. But at the same time they organised to eliminate by force any troublemakers who might take advantage of this seemingly liberal institutional reform. The increased political autonomy of the colonies, which benefited a small elite selected for its moderate character, was accompanied by the savage repression of popular movements that wanted to break the bonds of Franco-African dependence and were thus labelled as radicals.

The era of the 'modernisers': Roland Pré and Pierre Messmer

In Cameroon, this policy was pursued by two successive high commissioners in Yaoundé in the mid-1950s: Roland Pré, appointed in December 1954, and Pierre Messmer, who replaced him in April 1956. These two men in their forties, who had each fought in the Resistance against Nazism, were seen as modernisers.

A former mining engineer, Pré, who had previously held the post of governor in Gabon, Guinea and Upper Volta, was particularly interested in geostrategic and economic issues. A passionate anti-Communist, he dreamt of a mighty Eurafrique which, standing shoulder to shoulder with the United States, would be able to contend with the Soviet Union and China. In his view, this Cold War moment was not the time for national independence but for *inter*dependence among nations bound together in geostrategic 'great blocs'. In a break with his predecessors, Pré had no hesitation in talking about the autonomy or even the future independence of Cameroon. 'Formal independence is an outdated notion,' he explained in a circular to his subordinates in February 1955. The aim was not so much to combat nationalism as to 'control its expression [and] channel its aspirations' to make it compatible with the French-controlled 'European-African union' that Pré so desired.[2]

Pierre Messmer is today better known because of his later career, as he rose all the way to becoming prime minister. But at the time he was a less impressive figure. Educated in the 1930s at the National School of Overseas France, he joined the Free French Forces during the Second World War and spent the 1940s in Indochina (where he was briefly taken prisoner by the Viet Minh). This trusted fighter for the French colonial cause was appointed governor of Mauritania (1952–54) and then Côte d'Ivoire (1954–56). At the end of his stay in Abidjan – where Messmer worked hand in hand with Houphouët-Boigny, whose Franco-African philosophy he shared – Gaston Defferre hired him as chief of staff at the Ministry for Overseas France to finalise the drafting of the enabling law that would bear his name.

Pré and Messmer shared a keen interest in the new military doctrines developed by the French army in the 1950s. Defeated fifteen years earlier by the Nazis, it had suffered another humiliation at Diên Biên Phu in May 1954. Brought to its knees by the Viet Minh, which they had long, haughtily dismissed as a barefoot rabble, the French military hierarchy turned its attention to the theories developed by a new generation of officers who proposed a radical reform of combat doctrines. According to the young guard, war was not just a military conflict: it was a political, ideological and even psychological affair that involved the entire population. They now had to face a partisan army waging the revolutionary war preached by Mao Zedong, an army which blended in with the civilian population 'like a fish in water'. New warfare techniques thus needed to be developed.

As we noted in the introduction, this was the background to the development of the doctrine of revolutionary warfare (DRW). This doctrine, which was in fact *counter*revolutionary, proposed to subvert the enemy by imitating his methods. It can be summed up in three Ps. Firstly, it was a *preventive* war, designed to take action before the enemy (the fish) 'contaminated' the population (the water). Next, this was conceived as a *people's* war, since the aim was to force the population to defend itself against the enemy. Finally, this war was *psychological*, because the aim was not just to mobilise men physically, but to secure their conscious allegiance to the political-military authorities' political and ideological agenda.

The fundamentally antidemocratic nature of such a doctrine was not lost on its promoters. In a document entitled 'The Indochina Campaign;

Or a Lesson in "Revolutionary War"', partly published in *Le Monde* in August 1954, one of the main theorists of DRW, Colonel Charles Lacheroy, explained: 'The Viet Minh has developed a popular-political-police organisation, which is no doubt revolting to the human conscience, but also a weapon whose military effectiveness is unfortunately indisputable and, without doubt, decisive. Not to use it is to play a losing game.'[3]

1955: the strategy of shock

Reaching Cameroon in late 1954, Roland Pré had no intention of 'playing a losing game'. Describing the UPC as a Viet Minh in the making and a mere tentacle of the Cominform (the international Communist organisation controlled by the USSR), he immediately set in motion a vast plan to smother the 'Communist fish'. On 18 January 1955, he sent Lacheroy's pamphlet on revolutionary war to the entire local administration. On 4 February, moving from theory to practice, he sent out a circular telling colonial officials to implement Lacheroy's policy. In particular, this meant setting up what Lacheroy called 'parallel hierarchies' (youth organisations, women's groups, solidarity funds, village councils and so on) that would exert a physical, psychological and territorial grip on Cameroon's populations. The idea was to immunise them against Communism and encourage them to actively fight against the UPC's brand of 'subversion'.

Pré's offensive involved several moving parts. Its first aspect was socio-economic in nature: it sought to satisfy a limited set of social demands in order to stop the UPC from using them to their advantage. The second was psychological, consisting as it did of a vast propaganda operation. The press, traditional organisations and the Catholic hierarchy issued a steady stream of slogans hostile to the UPC, whose members were described as Communists, revolutionaries or diabolical atheists. Pré advocated a 'combative propaganda' which, he wrote, must be 'simple' and 'categorical' but also 'flexible' so that 'the mass of people to whom it is addressed can have the illusion of thinking for themselves [and so that] it is possible in all cases to disguise the origin, aims and means of the action undertaken'. The third, more directly repressive part of the plan set out to harass nationalist activists by combining judicial, administrative and police operations to prevent them from meeting, travelling, organising rallies or promoting their ideas – in short, from breathing. Numerous urban and village militias were discreetly set up by the French colonial administration to physically attack the UPC and to violently stop them from carrying out any form of activity.

This ultra-aggressive policy, which could be described as a strategy of tension or a strategy of shock, unsurprisingly set off a cycle of violence in Cameroon. Well aware of the trap set for them by Pré, the leaders of the UPC called on their supporters not to give in to provocation. Refusing to be intimidated, they decided to sharpen their slogans and step up their internal organisation. On 22 April 1955, the UPC and its sister organisations (the USCC, UDEFEC and JDC) published a Joint Proclamation calling for Cameroon's 'immediate independence'. This broke with the idea of an intermediate period in which the colonial power could prepare the way for independence. Indeed, the nationalists were concerned to avoid being caught out by the apparently liberal institutional reforms being prepared by the French government, which might captivate – or deceive – a section of Cameroonian public opinion.

Unsurprisingly, Pré interpreted the UPC's new demands as further proof of its subversive nature. In the days that followed, he deployed a heavy military presence – some of the troops came from Abidjan or Libreville – in the 'sensitive areas'. It was in this overheated atmosphere that a series of violent riots broke out in mid-May 1955. A result of the social discontent among the 'natives', constant provocation by the administration, and the harassment of protesters, the riots began in Mungo on 15 May. They then spread throughout the south of the territory – Douala, Yaoundé, Sanaga-Maritime, the Bamileke region and so on. The state apparatus moved immediately to violently repress the riots (see box below).

The riots of May 1955

Rioting in May 1955 produced an escalating spiral of violent confrontation between the UPC and the administration. In the space of just a few days, police harassment turned into full-scale military repression.

At Mbanga, Mungo, a banned UPC demonstration was forcibly dispersed by the gendarmerie on three successive occasions on 15, 16 and 22 May. On the last of these three, activists fought back. Following violent clashes with the police, the latter mounted a series of arrests and carried out combing operations in neighbourhoods known to favour the UPC. As a direct result of this repression, demonstrators targeted the prisons of Nkongsamba on 24 May and Loum the following day. In Loum, the prison was ransacked and the police fired on the crowd, killing six people, according to official sources. Three demonstrators were killed in the same way on 29 May in Tombel.

In Douala, rioting began on 22 May in the New Bell district, the birthplace of the UPC, when the authorities tried to establish a pro-French party called the National Front. Unsurprisingly, this provocation led to clashes between the nationalists and the two platoons of gendarmes dispatched to the area. Two days later, to back up the repressive efforts, Pré called in soldiers from all over French Africa and introduced a curfew. The next day, the riot spread to the New Bell prison. Supported by two tank platoons, the repression was devastating: after several hours of gunfire, the official toll was seven dead and around sixty injured. In this explosive context, two European civilians were killed in circumstances that have never been clarified. On 27 May, the UPC headquarters were set on fire, an act that the administration blamed on . . . the UPC itself. This implausible theory accused the nationalist organisation of seeking to 'stir up public opinion with a spectacular act'. Its Bafoussam and Bafang headquarters also went up in smoke.

The unrest eventually spread to Yaoundé on 26 May, when demonstrators ransacked the central police station to free comrades of theirs who had been arrested following an altercation between pro- and anti-UPC trade unionists. It was then that what the authorities called a stray bullet, fired from the police station, killed an African, outraging the activists who carried the corpse to the gates of the Territorial Assembly and then the next day to the central hospital, where the police fired on the crowd, killing three more people. The two weeks of conflict included numerous clashes and cases of score-settling involving the police and their auxiliaries, which remain poorly documented to this day. This makes it difficult to draw up an overall casualty count, beyond the official figure of twenty-two dead, and the more unofficial figure of fifty dead and one hundred and fifty wounded, mentioned in a confidential report.

Eliminating the UPC

These riots, whose form and spread conformed to a relatively classic pattern, immediately provided the French authorities and their local allies with a pretext to strike down their opponents. 'Current events should cause UPC's disappearance [from the] political scene [and] facilitate setting up of new structures,' noted Pré on 30 May in a telegram to the ministry which had oversight over him.[4]

Away from the public eye, the villages and districts deemed subversive were thoroughly combed by police and pro-French militias, in a repressive effort which claimed an unknown number of victims. While local UPC headquarters were methodically burnt down, traditional chiefs took advantage of the situation to liquidate their opponents in the localities they governed. 'We have seen ransacking, burning and unscrupulous evictions,' reported one Bamileke notable, despite his hostility to the UPC.[5] 'Some chiefs will shoot their subjects as if they were hunting game.' On 31 May, a dozen Cameroonian civil servants wrote anonymously to the UN secretary general: 'At the time of writing, the main centres in Cameroon are ablaze and steeped in blood. Hundreds of corpses, shot in broad daylight or in the greatest secrecy in the middle of the night, are being incinerated so that [no] trace of them will remain. The hospitals are packed out with the numbers of wounded and arrests have continued without respite.'[6]

More than eight hundred activists were rounded up and, in most cases, violently beaten up in police stations. Thousands more, hunted down by the authorities, headed onto the underground: the maquis. Blamed by both the colonial administration and the press for the unrest, the UPC's leaders had to go into hiding. General Secretary Ruben Um Nyobè took refuge in the scrubland in his native Sanaga-Maritime region. The organisation's president Félix Moumié fled to British Cameroon, disguised as a woman and riding a moped. In the British zone, he settled in Kumba, where he linked up with the UPC's vice-presidents Ernest Ouandié and Abel Kingué and most of the movement's other cadres.

The riots were a result of Pré's policies, but above all were used as a pretext to 'legally' eliminate the UPC from the Cameroonian political scene. While the hunt for UPC activists continued in the forest, officials from the Ministry of Overseas France scrutinised the high commissioner's biased reports to find legal justifications to break up the Cameroonian nationalist party. Having first brought the matter up on 15 January 1955 (though a ban on the UPC had already been discussed before that point) authorities resorted to a 1936 law, adopted in a very different context, which provided for the banning of movements that used 'combat groups' and 'private militias'. The decree officially banning the UPC, JDC and UDEFEC was signed by Prime Minister Edgar Faure (1908–88) on 13 July 1955.

Six months after wishing Pré 'a warm welcome and a happy New Year, in the hope that this year will see the dawn of Cameroon's independence',[7] Um Nyobè's party faced a particularly dangerous moment. Its leaders were in clandestinity or in exile; its activists were hunted down or in prison; its allies both at home and in France itself – informed only through official channels – were ever fewer in number. The situation was no better on the international stage. Barred from the RDA by Houphouët-Boigny on 9 July 1955, the UPC received very little support from the socialist countries, which lost interest in a movement that was ultimately Communist only in its enemies' imagination. Nor could it rely on the support of the independent states and nationalist movements which, meeting in Bandung (Indonesia) in April 1955, were only just beginning to make the voice of the 'Third World' heard. Worse still, the official ban deprived the UPC of a platform at the United Nations and of its favourite weapon: international law. In any case, this was the decision of the members of the UN visiting mission, on an inspection tour of Cameroon in October 1955: they would receive 'only representatives of legally established organisations'.

Crowning all these difficulties, the UPC also had to deal with its opponents stealing its political clothes – with the blessing of French authorities who had become much less hostile to 'nationalism' now that they had eliminated the only party that had consistently upheld this agenda since 1948. So continued the now-long-standing policy of sham political fronts. This can be seen during the campaign for the French parliamentary election held on 2 January 1956: while the UPC was barred from running, many candidates in the second electoral college cast themselves as various kinds of nationalist in order to attract voters. But once they had made it to the National Assembly in Paris, the lucky candidates – Jules Ninine, Alexandre Douala Manga Bell and André-Marie Mbida – immediately reverted to wiser pro-French sentiments. Of course, this ploy was no problem for Roland Pré, who, focused on his grand plans for Eurafrique, saw nationalism as nothing more than a propaganda tool. When he left Cameroon in April 1956, his final report advocated 'nurturing a moderate nationalism' and even taking up 'if necessary the term "independence"'.[8] Properly framed, such nationalism would, in his view, allow for an independent Cameroon to be integrated into an interdependent Franco-African (or Euro-African) bloc.

1956: the ambush, and the war

Indeed, taking over from Pré in April 1956, Pierre Messmer's aim was to properly channel Cameroonian nationalism in order to make it compatible with the plans prepared by Paris when it drew up the enabling law. The idea of this law, of which he was one of the main authors, was to liberalise colonial governance (allowing universal suffrage, decentralisation and so on) while reasserting France's control over its African domain (in particular by strengthening the links of economic and strategic interdependence). In the words of Gaston Defferre, it was a question of 'offering something to avoid a catastrophe'.[9]

In practical terms, the aim of the new high commissioner was to get the Cameroonians themselves to rubber-stamp their integration into the Franco-African system of interdependence. To achieve this, he announced two important decisions: the election by universal suffrage of a new local assembly and the adoption of an amnesty law for the 'agitators' of May 1955. These two complementary promises were consciously designed as an ambush: the amnesty was, in Messmer's own words, simply a 'means of influencing the UPCists, who will know that illegal agitation can only compromise their amnesty and their return'.[10] Messmer was in control of the timetable for this whole process, which he only gradually made official during 1956, and suggested to the independentists that they would be able to take part in the election, as candidates or voters, so long as they adopted a calm demeanour and abandoned the UPC label. The trap worked perfectly. While the UPC leadership wrangled over what strategy to adopt, Messmer announced that the elections would be held on 23 December, while maintaining the uncertainty surrounding the amnesty law, which would not finally be voted on until 11 December, after the electoral roll had already been closed.

Cornered, the UPC leadership abandoned the non-violent approach that Um Nyobè had hitherto held in place, including among his comrades who had taken refuge in Kumba. These latter were now increasingly tempted by a Vietnamese- or Algerian-style insurrectionary approach. Félix Moumié, for example, wrote to one of his French lawyers in February 1956:

[Our French friends] only seem to be really interested in a colonial problem as long as there is bloodshed. As you can understand, it's unthinkable that the lives of thousands of our brothers sacrificed in the cause of freedom should go unnoticed because in our country there is no problem of rebels or fellaghas. It's not our fault that we do not have the same privilege as our Maghrebian brothers to have the weapons to create a hotbed of terrorism here.[11]

On 2–3 December 1956, at a meeting in Makai, Sanaga-Maritime, the UPC decided to turn to armed action. A paramilitary organisation was set up to derail the electoral process: the National Organising Committee (CNO). Since the CNO did not have military-grade weapons, the goal of the 'active boycott' was not so much to bring

France to its knees as to grab the attention of international opinion. At 6 p.m. on 18 December 1956, the first actions were set in motion: candidates were physically assaulted, polling stations were attacked, bridges were sabotaged and hundreds of trees were cut down to block the roads. While in most regions the results were rather mixed, these actions did achieve their intended goal in two constituencies in Sanaga-Maritime, Um Nyobè's stronghold. In these electoral districts, which were the focus of the nascent uprising, the colonial administration was forced to cancel the election.

The French reaction was immediate. At the end of December, a military operation of unprecedented scale was launched in Sanaga-Maritime. Paratroopers landed in Eseka on Messmer's orders and an 'order-maintenance zone' was established for two months. The repression, which mobilised African troops from various colonies and relied on countless local militias, far exceeded the violence of the initial insurrection. On 31 December in particular, the *maquisards* who had just attacked a Catholic rally were spotted in the bush by French soldiers at Ekite, near Edea. '[They] could have driven the rebels out,' reported the administrator Philippe Antoine, who was leading the troops, 'but they preferred to fire into the thicket where the maquisards were hiding. For fifteen minutes, until I asked the officer to halt the shooting.'[12] A report by the French army stated that the repressive effort had killed fifty-six insurgents, not counting 'other corpses of rebels killed in the forest but never found'.[13]

This 'butchery', as a Protestant pastor put it at the time, was just one episode among many. 'Since 24 December, several localities in the Sanaga-Maritime region have been subjected to large-scale war operations,' Ruben Um Nyobè wrote in a text dated 3 January 1957:

Entire villages were completely looted and burnt, and livestock was systematically slaughtered with rifle fire. The furniture and the doors and windows of the houses were used as firewood for the troops' cooking. When the 'forces of order' arrived in each village or town, they fired on the defenceless population at point-blank range, without warning. Those who escaped this mass slaughter were chased into the bush by the 'forces of order' guided by a few [Cameroonian] traitors. Any adults or children they met along the way were shot dead by the soldiers without any form of trial. People caught in their homes were shot in cold blood by colonialist troops made up of French soldiers and Chadian riflemen from the so-called French Equatorial Africa (AEF). Each time, the killing was followed by the looting of property and the burning of houses. Men, women and children, coldly murdered by the bearers of 'civilisation', were thus left to rot in the bush. There is no one to count them and no one to bury them, as required by the most imperative of African customs.[14]

Kamerun, a Nation 'in the Maquis'

The official ban on the UPC in July 1955, the rigged election of December 1956 and the ensuing French military offensive brought about what might be called two parallel worlds in Cameroon. The first was the one visible on the official political scene, the stage for the politicians who accepted the rules of the French game, notwithstanding their declared nationalism. Its epicentre was the new Legislative Assembly, the ALCAM, which rubber-stamped the provisions of the Defferre enabling law almost without challenge. A real shadow play in which only secondary issues were debated, the legal political scene served as a springboard for those aspiring to greatness. In 1957, André-Marie Mbida won the colonial power's favour: he became the first head of government of Cameroon, which had legally become a 'trusteeship state' (if nominally an autonomous one) following the implementation of the Defferre enabling law.

But there was also a second Cameroon, made up of the tens of thousands of men and women who headed into the underground (or into exile) after the events of 1955–56. This was the submerged part of

Cameroonian politics, which, from November 1955, the UPC renamed Kamerun to signal their dissent from the official Cameroon, which had been usurped by 'puppets', and their desire to reunify the country according to the borders set during the era of German rule. This maquis counter-society was not just a pipe dream. Particularly well organised in Sanaga-Maritime, Ruben Um Nyobè's stronghold, it was made up of a civilian maquis, coordinated by an administrative secretariat/liaison office (SA/BL), and a military maquis, under the CNO's high command.

While the CNO's fighters had strong roots on the ground and enjoyed undeniable popularity, their efforts as a guerrilla force were undermined by a cruel lack of weapons. Equipped with machetes, knives and clubs, the Cenois – as the CNO fighters were known – had only a handful of pistols and cobbled-together rifles. The CNO fulfilled a dual function, as best as it could: protecting the civilian organisation against assaults by the colonial army and mounting offensives against the 'lackeys' who collaborated with the French administration. These operations were not launched blindly but by the decision of underground people's courts.

The dynamics of the insurgency are often hard to grasp since there is so much hybridisation between local and national motivations in each region, in each armed group and even within each individual maquisard. Take the Bamileke region, where there was less of a structured maquis organisation than in Sanaga-Maritime but where social life was built on a powerful web of chiefdoms. Here, the resistance was organised around a few young, traditional chiefs, including Pierre Kamdem Ninyim (Baham), Marcel Feze (Badenkop) and Jean-Rameau Sokoudjou (Bamendjou), who were closer to UPC circles. This alliance between traditional circles and revolutionary movements explains the strength of the insurrection that developed in this region in 1956.

The alliance was particularly pertinent in the chiefdom of Baham, the epicentre of the revolt. The son of the chief, Pierre Kamdem Ninyim, was called back from his studies in Paris in 1954 to succeed his father. But the young man, who had initially been nurtured by the colonial administration, had become an anticolonialist in metropolitan France through his contact with the progressive Federation of Black African Students in France (FEANF) and the Association of Cameroonian Students (AEC). Back home, he welcomed nationalist militants into his chiefdom, which led to him being charged in November 1956 with 'reconstituting a disbanded league' (that is, the UPC). He was subsequently deposed on 23 February 1957 and sentenced to two years' imprisonment on 12 March. In this same authoritarian vein, he was officially replaced at the head of his chiefdom by a substitute of disputed legitimacy. This sparked clashes between supporters of the deposed chief and those of the administration's own protégé.

This *coup de force*, seen as an unspeakable affront to tradition and as further proof of arbitrary colonial rule, fuelled closer unity between traditional and nationalist circles. This led, in October 1957, to the establishment of a new armed structure with a strange name: the Sinister of National Defence (SDN). Led by the large Baham diaspora and carried into other chiefdoms vexed by the colonial administration's various intrusions and injustices, the revolt spread like wildfire to the rest of the Bamileke region and to Mungo, home to a large Bamileke diaspora.

Drawing its resources and legitimacy from local traditions, this insurrection was mainly the work of UPC activists. It is particularly worth mentioning one of these activists from Badenkop, a young man in his twenties: Martin Singap. Head of the JDC and editor of the UPC newspaper *Lumière* during this party's legal period, Singap would play a central role in the nationalist army structures from 1957 onwards. Relying on the UPC organisations that had gone underground in 1955, these cadres tried to ensure coordination between the maquis in the various regions. However, this coordination was made difficult, if not impossible, by the French authorities' relentless repressive efforts.

1957–58: pacification in Sanaga-Maritime

In 1957, Cameroon descended into a violence from which it would not soon re-emerge – or, as French military hierarchs put it: Cameroon descended into war. 'The search, pursuit, capture and destruction of localised and identified armed bands no longer constitute an operation to restore order, but a "war operation,"' noted General Louis Dio, senior commander of the armed forces in the AEF-Cameroon defence zone, on 30 April 1957.[15] For his part, Daniel Doustin, a civilian political official in southern Cameroon and Messmer's right-hand man, warned: 'We are in danger of blithely heading towards a smaller version of Algeria.'[16]

That was just what happened in 1957. This was not so much because of the nationalist resistance: after all, while it was particularly combative and well organised, this movement had almost no weapons. Rather, it resulted from the determination of the French authorities who, seeking to eradicate the UPC once and for all, adopted the same methods as in Algeria. In any case, this was the thrust of Messmer's decision when he gave the go-ahead for a joint civilian-military operation directly inspired by the doctrine of revolutionary war: the creation of the Sanaga-Maritime Pacification Zone (ZOPAC).

Two men were at the helm of ZOPAC. On the civilian side was Daniel Doustin (1920–2004), who can be considered the father of the 'policy of shock'. A former information-bureau director in Indochina and then head of the Nyong-et-Sanaga region, this tactically astute administrator had initially regretted the trap set by Messmer for the UPC. This had been a 'mistake', Doustin wrote in a secret report, which had 'pitched the UPC towards a violent solution'.[17] But once the mistake had been made, Doustin felt it necessary to plough ahead – and engage in a violent showdown. On the military side, it was a theorist of the doctrine of revolutionary war, Lieutenant-Colonel Jean Lamberton

(1911–2004), who took command. Like all those who implemented this strategy in Cameroon, the Indochina War had left its mark on him personally, and he now sought revenge in the heart of Africa.

Together, they created the Pacification Zone, which was limited both in time (from December 1957 to December 1958) and in space, restricted as it was to the Sanaga-Maritime region. An exceptional regime was established there, in the name of striking at the heart of the insurrection. Seven parachute companies from French Equatorial Africa were placed at Lamberton's disposal, totalling some 1,500 men. As in the Battle of Algiers, which had been launched a few months previously, all the lessons of the doctrine of revolutionary war were put to use in the battle over the ZOPAC. This meant cordoning off the territory, dividing it up into districts and sub-districts, deporting whole populations to resettlement camps, mobilising combat militias, extrajudicial executions, psychological warfare efforts, forced disappearances, torture and many other such tools.

The first phase in the creation of the ZOPAC, prior to the other operations, was the forced resettlement of populations in closely guarded villages which had been created from scratch by the French army. This was a typical feature of (counter)revolutionary war, from the first experiments of this kind in Cambodia in 1952 to Algeria starting in 1956 – not forgetting the British army's 'villagisation' strategy in the Kikuyu Reserves in Kenya.[18] In the space of a few weeks, a large part of Sanaga's population was uprooted from its usual settings in a dispersed habitat and resettled instead along the main roads behind barbed-wire walls. The method was both simple and brutal: crops were ripped up and villages destroyed in order to force the now-destitute inhabitants to seek protection from the authorities. Forced to choose between the maquis and the camp, the region's inhabitants were thereby transformed into a refugee population. Those who did come to the fortified villages were herded into makeshift huts, which relied on the French army for their supplies. The people were closely monitored, with a pass required for every move. Inside the camps, the huts were numbered; a roll-call could be made at any moment in order to flush out any individuals who might have absented themselves to join the maquis. The villagers were also bombarded with slogans designed to 'psychologically turn' the resettled populations. Lamberton's propaganda repeated that 'UPC is a tik-tik fly; it stings, it puts you to sleep, it kills'. Or likewise: 'In the forest lurk the wild beast and the criminal.'[19]

The rest of the territory, which was not similarly under army control, was declared a 'prohibited area': anyone found there was ipso facto to be considered an outlaw and treated as such. Military patrols and militias were sent into these 'infested zones' to track down and eliminate the rebels. With unscrupulous leaders like Pierre Dimala and Jacques Bidjoka, these auxiliary forces brought a reign of terror. Greatly familiar with Bassa territory and society, they struck hard blows against the CNO and committed abuses on a mass scale, much to the satisfaction of the French officers. The latter were content to reap the results of this invisible war, which had the added advantage of costing France particularly little in terms of resources, and turned a blind eye to the methods used. For instance, when Bidjoka was arrested in 1961 under the accusation of murdering a police prefect, Bidjoka confessed to having 'killed more than six hundred people under pressure from the colonialists', specifically by dropping them into the River Sanaga.[20]

In accordance with the fundamentals of DRW, in 1958 the French officers in the Pacification Zone high command and their Cameroonian auxiliaries waged a war to gather intelligence. Torture was used extensively for this purpose, particularly by the policeman Georges Conan, the all-powerful director of the Eseka special commissariat – an especially 'brutal' officer, as Lamberton called him in his personal notes. However, the police were not the only ones with a taste for interrogation, as Roland Barachette, administrative head of the Sanaga-Maritime region at the end of 1958, later explained. Referring to a 'section that had just returned from Algeria', headed by a 'French para-trooper lieutenant', he said: 'They did the questioning like in Algeria, using the bathtub method. They had picked up some bad habits.'[21]

September 1958: the elimination of Ruben Um Nyobè

After a few months of operations, the French authorities bit by bit managed to impose 'order' on the Sanaga-Maritime region. The CNO had been hurriedly established at the end of 1956; now weakened, isolated and poorly equipped, it was unable to withstand the blows of the French army and its auxiliaries. Not only did the latter enjoy a numerical advantage, but they were also ready to commit any number of atrocities. If even in this sense the odds were stacked against the insurgents, it is still worth noting yet another imbalance that helped the French: the unequal information war.

The theorists and practitioners of the doctrine of revolutionary war recognised that 'modern warfare' was above all a political, ideological and psychological war, and so they paid particular attention to handling public opinion. Considered a specialist in psychological warfare (he taught a course on the topic at the École supérieure de guerre in Paris in 1955), Lamberton did everything he could to filter the information that reached France. 'There must be no talk about what is happening in Sanaga-Maritime,' he wrote in March 1958. 'So far we have succeeded – we must ensure silence.'[22]

While France's propaganda in the resettlement camps had little impact on the local populations, the blackout in which it cloaked its military operations did prove particularly effective. Unlike in Algeria, where even during the war the French army's methods were the subject of intense debate back home, the drama unfolding in Cameroon went completely unnoticed.

Apart from the Communist press, which published a few articles based on the scant information that did make it to France, the only newspapers that took an interest were the ones that spread French military propaganda. They congratulated the army's efforts against the 'rebel bands' in Cameroon, who were invariably described as a ragbag of irredeemable and bloodthirsty 'savages', gorging on 'Communism' and 'witchcraft'. Dissenting voices in Cameroon or France that tried to tell a different story were systematically silenced. Such was the case of the Cameroonian newspaper *L 'Opinion*, whose editor, Marcel Bebey-Eyidi, was imprisoned on 23 December 1957 for 'reconstituting a disbanded league'. Then there was the pamphlet *Na{isme et Attila au Kamerun*: distributed by the Federation of Black African Students in France, the copies were seized in June 1958.

With the UPC's resistance in Sanaga-Maritime losing ground from one day to the next, the noose tightened around Um Nyobè himself. The UPC leader was a formidable organiser who held considerable sway in the region and also had contacts abroad; and in the French army's view, the uprising's future success would depend on him personally. Hence, in a final report on the pacification of Sanaga-Maritime, Lamberton spoke of Um Nyobè in the following terms:

> In his uncomfortable and precarious maquis, he did a considerable job of work, always writing clear and precise instructions, newspaper articles, propaganda tracts and pamphlets, keeping up a hefty correspondence with UPC branches in Cameroon, Paris, Toulouse . . . with Cameroonian students abroad, with journalists in France and even the most minor militants in the Sanaga-Maritime region; discussing a point of organisation or doctrine with this or that one, keeping a polemic going with another; fuelling the faith of the humble and the *évolués*, whom he tirelessly endeavoured to instruct and convince.[23]

Such an enemy had to be eliminated. This was done in an operation on 13 September 1958, relying on information obtained by torturing a female prisoner. The physical elimination of the Cameroonian leader, carried out during an expedition to the prohibited area by a patrol of Cameroonian and Chadian soldiers led by French officers, offers a good illustration of DRW methods. So does the propaganda surrounding Um Nyobè's death: his body was dragged along the ground, paraded in public, photographed and then buried under a layer of concrete. The profanation of the body of the man who was regarded locally as a hero, even a prophet, was then extensively exploited throughout the country, in order to have the maximum psychological effect on the population. They were showered with leaflets announcing the death of the 'god who was wrong'. This had some success: in the weeks that followed, thousands of dejected maquisards came out of hiding and, with a heavy heart, came over to the government side. ZOPAC officially came to an end at the end of 1958.

In West Cameroon, 'just like in Algeria'

At the same time as 'pacifying' the Sanaga-Maritime region, Messmer began a crackdown on nationalists in the Bamileke region, widely known as West Cameroon. In the weeks following the creation of the SDN, renamed Sinister of National Defence of Kamerun (SDNK) in October 1957, anti-French attacks mounted, spreading throughout the region and into neighbouring Mungo. While Messmer did not create another pacification-zone apparatus akin to ZOPAC, he did launch a violent campaign of repression. He handed its leadership to a trusted ally who had been his colleague at the Ministry for Overseas France: Maurice Delauney (1919–2009).

As administrative head of the Bamileke region from June 1956 to December 1958, Delauney relied on hardline helpers who had already been initiated in the techniques of revolutionary warfare, such as his military adviser, the lieutenant Bonaventure Escoffet. A veteran of Indochina, Escoffet had been trained at what was then the temple of the DRW: the Military Centre for Overseas Information and Specialisation (CMISOM), headed by Colonel Lacheroy. There, Escoffet met another of Delauney's adjuncts: the young Samuel Kamé. Originally from the highly sensitive chieftaincy of Baham, Kamé was part of the first generation of Cameroonians who studied in France after the Second World War, including at Sciences Po Paris and the National School of Overseas France (ENFOM). A specialist in the delicate issue of Bamileke chieftaincies, he helped French administrators to understand the local political system – and how best to manipulate it.

Delauney did not have the same resources as Lamberton, and his men delegated some of the work to the chiefs and their servants, the *tchindas*, who were given carte blanche to settle scores with their local opponents. Like Joseph Kamga, chief of Bandjoun, these loyalist chiefs engaged in a fight to the death with the rebels – thereby also tying their own fate to France. On the other hand, chiefs who opposed France or were simply considered too soft suffered fierce repression. Such was the case of nationalist chief of Bamendjou, Jean-Rameau Sokoudjou. His chiefdom was militarily occupied between November 1957 and June 1958, and his wives were raped right in front of him by Cameroonian soldiers (under French command).

Rape, pillage, arson, murder, emasculations, public executions . . . A long list of abuses were committed during the so-called Bamileke civil war, which was in fact orchestrated by the French authorities. The war was all the murkier given that the different sides involved here were less clearly defined than in Sanaga-Maritime. With some chiefs changing allegiance according to circumstances, and some maquis clearly infiltrated and sometimes secretly turned over by their adversaries, locals took refuge in a deafening silence. This itself enraged the French authorities, who were obsessed with 'intelligence gathering'.

The systematic use of torture

An eminent professor of literature in the United States, Ambroise Kom was around ten years old in 1959 when the French army came to occupy the dispensary in Batié where his uncle, a nurse, was working. 'The army would bring resistance fighters back there, and the operations to extract information from them were carried out in the open air,' he explained when we met him in 2011.

> Torture was also carried out in full view. It was there for the first time that I saw the 'swing': two stakes in the ground and a crossbar that was used to hang the subject, with his feet and hands tied. I think they poured something that looked like petrol up his nose and spun him around. This allowed the army to extract some confessions or information. This happened all the time, practically daily. Every time the army brought someone back, you had to go through this experience.

Torture, practised by the Franco-Cameroonian forces, was a constant throughout the war in Cameroon. It was the shared fate of all the rebel leaders who passed through their hands. For example, the former rebel leader in the Centre region, Henri Tamo, was tortured in Yaoundé in 1957: he was subjected to simulated drowning and beaten with a bicycle chain, the marks of which were still visible on his body when we met him some fifty years later. Arrested in Sangmélima in the summer of 1959 and also sent to Yaoundé, one of his close friends, Samuel Zeze, secretary general of the high command of the Centre Military Territory (TMC) – the branch of the CNO in the Yaoundé region – suffered even worse. As he told us in 2007: 'They tie you up like this, a stick here. It's extremely painful. And at the same time, they plug in an electric wire and tell you, "If you confess, we'll get you down again. Otherwise you'll die here." I knew two people in the Yayap camp who weren't even UPC men, but who are today in their graves.'

The succession of accounts shows that there were indeed many acts of torture, but they do not prove a political determination to use torture systematically. This is where the recollections of Jean-Paul Martin – president in 1959 of the court in the Mungo capital, Nkongsamba – are instructive. Meeting us in Paris in 2008, this former French magistrate told us that gendarmes had handed over a UPC liaison officer:

> I realised that he had been tortured by what appeared to be two French gendarmes in the region. In my office, this young man showed me his cigarette scars on his chest and back. He told me that two French brigadiers had made him talk with the help of a *gégène* [a small electric generator attached to electrodes].

Deciding to open an investigation, he came under pressure from Georges Maîtrier, captain of the gendarmes in Cameroon, and ended up being expelled from Cameroonian territory by Prime Minister Ahidjo's – French – chief of staff. By preventing the colonial justice system from investigating a proven act of torture, the highest political and military authorities demonstrated that their main concern was to conceal the systematic use of the practice.

As in the Sanaga-Maritime region, torture had a key role in the arsenal from which the 'forces of order' drew. When we conducted our investigation half a century later, there were still many witnesses, both French and Cameroonian, who could tell us about the techniques used: 'swings', waterboarding, leg irons and so on. 'Delauney's method was repression at all costs,' a colonial administrator working in the region in 1957 explained to us in 2009. 'You arrest people, you make them talk, and it's never-ending, just like in Algeria.'[24]

Torture – practised behind closed doors or in the open air in chiefly courts or in front of gendarmerie stations – was perfectly acceptable to the authorities. Take the case of one specialist in torture, Georges Maîtrier, the French commander of the Dschang gendarmerie squadron. After a few months of operations, he was congratulated by his superiors for having neutralised 'several hundred outlaws' and having 'led a merciless fight against subversive elements' in the region.[25]

Much as in Algeria, where the French army had in this moment developed the habit of throwing rebels into the sea from helicopters (the famous 'Bigeard's shrimps'), enforced disappearances were also on the rise in West Cameroon. The gigantic waterfalls that pockmark this hilly region served as giant tombs: at night, the French gendarmes got rid of their enemies by throwing them into the racing water alive. Sometimes too alive, as French gendarme André Houtarde found out on 12 September 1959, when he was carried along by his victim as he threw him into the immense Metche Falls to the northwest of Bafoussam.

The outlaws who did not die by torture, bullets or waterfalls were kept in an unofficial internment camp set up in April 1958 near Bangou. Delauney considered the colonial law too lax and decided to secretly intern all those whom he deemed accomplices to the insurgents. '[In this camp], I had perhaps seven or eight hundred people who were incarcerated, who stayed there for quite a while,' he explained in 2005, a few years before his death. 'You know, I had been a prisoner in Germany for a while, so I knew how it worked! So I set up a camp, with barbed wire and watchtowers.'[26]

French–British tensions

Behind the bloody war between Cameroonian nationalists and French colonialists, a more muted battle was being waged between the French and British authorities. The old colonial rivalries between Paris and London were being played out locally – and as France cracked down on its Cameroonian adversaries, it despaired of the passivity of the British on their side of the border. The British authorities, who administered the strip of Cameroonian territory between French Cameroon and Nigeria, found themselves unwillingly involved in the conflict when the UPC activists outlawed and hunted down in the French zone from 1955 sought refuge on the British side of the border.

The French soon requested that their British counterparts either suppress the UPC escapees or hand them over. But the British had no legal basis to do so and no particular desire to import the conflict into their territory. The UPC had, after all, used it only as a sanctuary, without carrying out any armed activities in the British zone. The French thus resorted to strange methods to get round their neighbour and to ramp up the pressure on the British. As he later told General de Gaulle, the minister for overseas France, Gaston Defferre, went so far as to travel to London in 1956 to threaten his British counterparts that if they did not cooperate in the fight against the UPC, the French would stir up trouble in Britain's colonies! A few months later, in April 1957, it was Delauney who tried to act tough: he launched a secret operation against the UPC infrastructure in Bamenda, British Cameroon. One night, a French–Cameroonian commando destroyed the UPC headquarters there and murdered the UPC activist Irénée Taffon and his wife in their sleep.

The French pressure finally paid off. On 4 June 1957, the UPC was banned in British territory as well. Its leaders were imprisoned and then deported to Sudan. For Moumié, Ouandié, Kingué and the others, this was the start of an exile lasting several years, which took them successively to Khartoum, Cairo, Accra and Conakry. This nomadic existence took them from their country, and hampered coordination with the maquis back home. The banning of the UPC was not, however, enough to prevent the Cameroonian nationalist party from maintaining a base in British Cameroon: in June, a new movement was formed, the One Kamerun Party, whose founder Ndeh Ntumazah made no secret of his closeness to the UPC. For years, he acted as intermediary between the UPC leadership in exile and the fighters in the interior.

Although the British cooperated with the French authorities – eventually handing over the 'terrorists' that their counterparts demanded – their confidential reports showed a certain unease about what they called the 'bestiality' of French methods.[27] In July 1958, a civil servant complained to the French consul in Lagos that the people handed over to the French were, 'in the presence of our own officers, immediately subjected to violence'.[28] Others took offence at the fact that extradited UPC activists were tortured and subjected to summary trials. Such was the case of Pierre Simo, head of the SDNK, who was handed over by the British at the end of 1958 and executed in Bafoussam town square in July 1959.

But for all the fuss they made in their confidential reports, the British steered well clear of expressing this indignation in public. Fearing that French Cameroon would descend into chaos or, worse still, into Communism, they preferred to maintain a complicit silence. And anyway, weren't these French methods rather like the British army's own counterinsurgency techniques used to crush the Mau Mau in 1950s Kenya?

4

Stolen Independence (1959–60)

The fruit of our historic conquest has just been snatched away by
an outright coalition of international imperialism. Our enemies at
home and abroad are determined, and will use independence as a
new means of subjecting our country to foreign domination.
— Letter sent from the UPC Information Office
in Rabat, 14 March 1959

Despite what official propaganda claimed in heated years of conflict, the UPC leaders were no cranks. In fact, a look at France's political, diplomatic and military archives half a century later proves that the Cameroon nationalists saw exactly what Paris was up to. It was because Ruben Um Nyobè, Félix Moumié, Ernest Ouandié and their comrades showed such unfailing determination that their opponents could find no way of silencing them other than force – or murder.

In other territories, French officials managed to bring trouble-makers to heel by duping or buying them – sometimes in the most literal sense. But in the Cameroonian theatre they found themselves up against skilful strategists who, despite their meagre resources, managed to foil most of the traps set for them. In between the lines of the archives, some French officials even let slip a certain admiration for their enemies. Meanwhile their supposed greatest friends – the local allies lauded in the official press – are described in confidential reports as mere pawns.

Once the French leaders recognised they would have to grant Cameroonian independence, the battle over the meaning of independence, which began in 1958, was again the focus of a confrontation between the French and the UPC. This clash played out as much on the international stage as in the scrublands of Cameroon.

'Can we deny people happiness?'

What exactly is the point of a country being independent? Today, it seems so natural that the question is rarely even asked. But coming up with an answer is not as easy as it may seem; the word *independent* can conceal very different realities. For most leaders, independence first and foremost means birth of a nation-state, with its own borders and institutions recognised by the population and by other nations. For others, the concept of independence refers to a deeper reality: it expresses the will of a people which, free from any foreign tutelage, decides to create a framework within which the members of the community can freely choose their fate and enter into an equal dialogue with their foreign counterparts. These are, in short, the two distinct paths open to colonised countries and peoples when the moment of independence comes.

In French Africa, this debate began in earnest in the mid-1950s, the period in which French officials began to speak openly about the continent's path to independence. There were several factors driving this gradual change of tack. Firstly, there were domestic ones. As France fought a costly war in Indochina, French public opinion was increasingly sceptical of the value of the colonial system. This was also true of some business chiefs, who noted that the colonies were not as profitable as they had been made out to be. In 1953, Edmond Giscard d'Estaing – a leading exponent of colonial employers in his function as chairman of the Financial Company for France and the Overseas Territories (SOFO) – proposed the idea of a limited independence, as in Morocco and Tunisia. For him, 'limitations on the independence of associated states would have to be instituted at the very moment independence was granted; a status would have to be agreed, and guarantees of bases, ports and free zones would have to be secured by treaty'.[1]

France had been defeated at Diên Biên Phu in May 1954 and had to grant independence to Indochina, and the National Liberation Front (FLN) launched its uprising in Algeria just a few months later. In this context, the idea of independence for the colonies gained further ground in metropolitan France. In 1955, Paris negotiated the independence of the Tunisian and Moroccan protectorates, which was proclaimed in March 1956. In the columns of *Paris Match* the following summer, the journalist Raymond Cartier made a name for himself, as mentioned earlier, by denouncing the financial costs of colonisation. So-called Cartierism – summed up in the famous phrase 'la Corrèze avant le Zambèze' (put Corrèze before the Zambezi) – was all the better received given that the international situation seemed less hopeful for the colonial powers than ever. In November 1956, French and British troops, allied with the Israelis, were humiliated in the Suez crisis.

While allied in that conflict, the French and British were not on the same wavelength elsewhere on the continent. London, which was more far-sighted than Paris, did not close the door on negotiated independence processes in sub-Saharan Africa. This was particularly true of the Gold Coast, whose independence, announced in 1956, was officially proclaimed on 6 March 1957. The sovereignty of this new nation-state, which would be called Ghana, provoked a chain reaction in Togo and Cameroon. The part of Togo under British trusteeship, which had voted in favour of joining its neighbour Ghana in a UN-supervised referendum in May 1956, thus became independent of London rule. Forced to react, Paris organised a referendum on the subject in French Togo in October 1956, which gave the choice between maintaining the status of a territory under UN trusteeship or else autonomy within the French Union. But the ballot – which handed an overwhelming majority to the second option – was rebuffed by the UN General Assembly. Noting that the Togolese people had not been offered independence, the General Assembly decided that elections should be held under UN supervision. The vote, held in April 1958, saw the pro-independence Togolese Unity Committee (CUT) win an overwhelming majority. Its president, Sylvanus Olympio (1902–63), who the French deemed close to the British and Americans and who had been treated as a subversive and deprived of his civil rights just a few weeks earlier, became Togo's prime minister.

The developments in Togo also had repercussions in Cameroon, where the French authorities feared a similar scenario might play out. Added to this mix, the British had already announced the forthcoming independence of Nigeria, to which British Cameroon was administratively attached. Even as the repression raged on in Sanaga-Maritime, French strategists were also devising a political plan that would save them from being again caught out by the march of events. The idea was to find some ploy that could shepherd the country towards independence – now recognised as inevitable – while keeping it within the French fold.

It was Daniel Doustin, civilian chief of the ZOPAC, who formulated the French strategy in the most clear-sighted – and cynical – fashion. Noting the popularity of the call for independence among Cameroon's populations, he was one of the first to understand that this notion could paradoxically be used as a propaganda tool in the war on 'subversives'. 'This magic word draws its strength essentially from the fact that it is vague,' he wrote in a secret bulletin a week before the Togolese elections in April 1958. 'Independence is the freedom to do what you want, not to pay taxes, to charge the highest price for cocoa and palm kernels, etc., etc. Independence is happiness. Can we deny people happiness?' Since it was impossible to hold off this 'happiness' any longer, Doustin recommended to his superiors that they should take ownership of this 'magic word' and turn it against those who demanded independence most intransigently.[2]

This was the secret plan that took shape in 1958. In the same vein as the strategy rolled out by Roland Pré in 1955 – pulling the rug out from under the UPC by copying part of their slogans and barring them from the legal political field – French officials integrated the concept of independence into their official discourse. The aim: to divide the nationalist camp and neutralise the political struggle of its most radical wing. In this sense, there was a considerable shift in official propaganda. The conflict in Cameroon was not in fact being fought between the French authorities and the independence fighters, it explained, but between the supporters of 'peace' and the supporters of 'terrorism'. The former were no longer fighting against 'independence', noted Doustin in February 1958, 'we are fighting over what regime there will be'.[3] With independence in sight, everything must be done to ensure that Communists did not benefit.

France prepares a 'negotiated independence'

There was a lot of talk about the 'regime' at this time, both in Yaoundé and in Paris. In Yaoundé, the status of the trusteeship state, granted in 1957 by the Defferre enabling law, was outdated now that the French authorities were laying the groundwork for Cameroon's independence. In Paris, the Fourth Republic, shaken by the war in Algeria, was finally brought to its knees in May 1958. These two factors provided the context in which French authorities prepared their plan for a negotiated independence for Cameroon, which they intended to present to the UN in New York and thereby bring an end to the trusteeship.

But in order to negotiate, you need someone to negotiate with. Political life in the administrative capital of French Cameroon was in turmoil in 1958. In February, the erratic André-Marie Mbida resigned as prime minister. A few backroom manoeuvres were enough to get rid of Mbida, who was too fiery, too opportunistic and too tribal, and who no longer fitted the bill for the French. They wanted a more polished face for Cameroon's government, and the prime ministerial role was instead handed to Ahmadou Ahidjo. A native of North Cameroon and the head of a party that was still being set up, the Cameroon Union – a vehicle that helped him to rally northern elites behind him – Ahidjo was a faithful disciple of Louis-Paul Aujoulat, whom he had met during his studies in Paris. This thirty-five-year-old was surely not known for his charisma. The French who worked with Ahidjo most closely were even more dismissive of him; judging by what they had to say, his main quality was that he knew how to 'read and write'. But the real strong point of Prime Minister Ahidjo, who had only made it into the Legislative Assembly thanks to electoral chicanery, was his loyalty to France. 'Despite his weaknesses and his uncertain ambitions,' said a French officer in a confidential report, 'Ahidjo is the best – or the least bad – of Cameroon's politicians, both because of his gifts and because he seems willing to keep Cameroon in France's orbit.'[4]

It was with this man – supervised by the high commissioner, surrounded by French advisers, and assisted by a few Cameroonians trained in metropolitan France – that the colonial authorities were to 'negotiate' the gradual transition to independence. While de Gaulle, who had come to power in May 1958, managed to convince Sylvanus Olympio to postpone the immediate independence that he sought for Togo, Cameroon appeared to be the trial run in French Africa.

During a two-month stay in Paris in the summer of 1958, Ahidjo, standing alongside de Gaulle, expressed the 'desire of the Cameroonian people to move towards independence, with the help of France, and its hope of obtaining its sovereignty in order to freely associate with her [France]'.[5] Behind the carefully loaded words, French officials knew that their wager had been a success: Cameroon would remain 'associated' with France despite reaching an independent status. A month after Um Nyobè's assassination, High Commissioner Xavier Torré announced on the radio in Yaoundé that Cameroon would become independent on 1 January 1960, after a one-year transition.

General de Gaulle, brought back to power in May 1958 to prevent the loss of Algeria, saw that the situation there was slipping from his grasp and looked for halfway-house solutions that could keep the other African colonies in the French fold. Cameroon was seen as a trial run insofar as its gradual path to independence might foreshadow similar processes in francophone Africa. This transition meant an independence that would be bilaterally negotiated between French leaders and their local allies, and bound by firm ties of association with France. The concept of association was at the heart of the referendum held in each of France's remaining colonial territories on 28 September 1958, along with the parallel plebiscite held in metropolitan France itself the same day. While holding out the prospect of independence – which de Gaulle promised 'France will not oppose' – France's leadership called on Africans to endorse the French Community outlined in the Constitution of the Fifth Republic, up for the vote in that referendum. All these territories agreed, with the exception of Guinea. Under the influence of Sékou Touré (1922–84), who was well aware of the fool's bargain that the Gaullist regime was offering, Guinean voters overwhelmingly rejected this association pact which, as a premise for any further development, de facto ruined the promise of independence. 'There is no dignity without freedom,' said the Guinean leader during the referendum campaign. 'We prefer freedom in poverty to wealth in slavery.' Guinea gained its independence on 2 October 1958. France's eleven other African colonies obtained a halfway-house status: while granted an 'autonomous' government, their local leaders ceded to the French Community, led from Paris, the management of certain essential prerogatives such as defence, diplomacy and currency.

After the defeat in Indochina, the agonising Algerian question and the complications in Togo, the setback in Guinea heightened the French authorities' determination to win their gamble in Cameroon. To avoid the risk of the country drifting away from France, links with the Ahidjo government were tightened in the run-up to independence in January 1960. This was the purpose of the agreements and conventions signed with Ahidjo at the end of 1958, which applied to the autonomous State of Cameroon for the transitional year of 1959. They were negotiated between unequal partners – a sovereign state and a state under trusteeship – and in practice took the form of negotiations *between* Frenchmen (representatives of France on one side and Ahidjo's French advisers on the other). The resulting texts, which dealt with pivotal issues, drastically reduced Cameroon's autonomy, as a prelude to its future independence. Worse still, some of these agreements were signed in secret. This was notably true of a highly sensitive convention 'relating to defence, public order and the use of the gendarmerie', whose longest and most detailed article concerned 'mineral substances classified as defence materials'. These substances – oil, gas, uranium, thorium, lithium, beryllium and others – were thus effectively removed from the sovereign control of the former trustee state of Cameroon, for the Cameroonian prime minister had made a written commitment to refer to the French government if any dispute should emerge over the exploitation of these resources.[6]

Even such serious infringements of Cameroonian sovereignty did not seem to trouble local politicians, who had been carefully kept out of the French-'Cameroonian' negotiations. Instead, the country's looming independence offered attractive openings for Cameroonian politicians, who sought to flatter a colonial administration still in control of the legal political scene. The French authorities' internal reports tended to describe Cameroonian political life as a simple chess board;

all they needed to do was to move the pawns around – the main aim being to keep at bay the intransigent pro-independence forces. To this end, Doustin, ever the shrewd strategist, suggested that former rebels be brought back into the saddle through a selective amnesty policy. In February 1958, he wrote that it would be desirable to

> encourage, if possible discreetly, the formation on the left wing of Soppo Priso [the main legal opposition figure] of a political party made up of UPC dissidents . . . who had formally and publicly condemned terrorism and who, under another name, would take up the ideas of the UPC: independence and reunification.[7]

This was the scenario that took shape in the months following Um Nyobè's death. Following the reintegration of former UPC men who had rejected the armed struggle, such as Mathieu Tagny and Charles Assalé, even former maquisards who had rallied behind the colonial administration made their political comeback. Such was the case of Théodore Mayi Matip, who was the UPC secretary general's former right-hand man.

This political scene expressed only a false pluralism, built on a carefully studied ethnic balance (the Foulbé Ahidjo, the Douala Soppo Priso, the Bassa Mayi Matip, the Boulou Assalé, the Bamileke Tagny and so on). This was also a falsely democratic political scene, in which the main issue – the real content of the word *independence* – was never up for discussion. For instance, Mayi Matip, elevated to the rank of opposition leader and still claiming the legacy of Um Nyobè, expressed himself in terms similar to those of Ahidjo: 'Our long struggle for the independence of Cameroon has now been crowned with success,' he rejoiced. 'By 1 January 1960, our country will be independent and its application to join the UN will be supported by all nations.'[8]

The UPC pushes back against French plans

Faced with France's political and military offensive, the UPC did not give up. Since the organisation had been banned in French Cameroon in 1955 and in the British zone in 1957, the UPC took to the international stage. While acknowledging the French desire to lead Cameroon to independence, its leaders tried to convince their foreign interlocutors that this would only have real value if the Cameroonian people were consulted beforehand. They called for a referendum explicitly posing the question of independence and for UN-supervised elections that would allow all political forces – including the UPC – to compete and express themselves freely. Seeking to loosen the vice that was now tightening around a Cameroonian nation-state associated with Paris and orchestrated to serve French interests, the UPC sought to restore the real meaning of independence, which had been used by the French as a simple counter-subversive propaganda tool.

Given Cameroon's special status and given that the UPC had always adopted a pan-African and internationalist orientation, very early on, the organisation's leaders established contacts in other countries, in Africa and beyond. It maintained relations in France's other African colonies, despite its exclusion from the RDA in July 1955. But it was especially after the ban in the British zone, where most of the party's leadership had taken refuge, that it built up its international contacts.

Initially exiled in Sudan, the Bureau of the Steering Committee (BCD) of the nationalist party found a new home in Egypt. Cairo, where the first conference of the Solidarity Council of the Afro-Asian Countries (later, AAPSO) was held in December 1957, became the exiled UPC's operational base. Financially supported by AAPSO's permanent secretariat, it set up an office in the Egyptian capital, which enabled it to deepen its relations with other national liberation movements, such as the Algerian FLN and Morocco's Istiqlal, whose newspapers echoed the party line of the Kamerun fighters' struggle. As well as taking advantage of Egypt's powerful radio transmitters – which enabled them to broadcast their propaganda as far as Cameroon – the UPC most importantly benefited from new facilities for printing their newspaper, *La Voix du Kamerun*, and numerous pamphlets documenting, with photos, France's doings in Cameroon.

Cairo also became the base from which UPC activists travelled to any city around the world where they could get a hearing: Damascus for the conference of Afro-Asian jurists, Stockholm for the World Peace Conference, and New York for hearings before the UN Trusteeship Council. Over in Geneva, Ernest Ouandié tried to make the International Council of the Red Cross (ICRC) aware of the arbitrary detentions and torture endured by the people of Cameroon. Having initially shown some concern over the matter, the Red Cross leadership eventually closed the case. It had sought explanations from Paris, only for the French government to convince it that sending a mission to Cameroon was hardly necessary given that the country was about to become independent.[9]

In its own way, this Red Cross response illustrates the growing gulf of misunderstanding that separated the Cameroonian nationalists from their potential European supporters. Now that the country was officially en route to independence, these potential supporters struggled to understand the nationalists' continued attitude of protest. Like the former UPC activists who had rallied to the administration's side and refused to open their eyes to what French-defined independence really involved, many European anticolonial activists – including even the most committed former supporters of Um Nyobè – disapproved of Moumié's violent strategy. They could understand that the Algerians had to fight for their independence, but why did Cameroonian nationalists who had secured independence already not negotiate with France, as their counterparts in Togo had? There were many reasons for such incomprehension: these anticolonial activists had been kept in the dark about the situation in Cameroon, misinformed by Franco-British propaganda, and were sometimes blinded by their own paternalistic certainties – often they were quite simply unaware that the UPC had repeatedly sought a peaceful solution (only for Moumié's confidential letters to the French and British authorities to go unanswered). For all these reasons, they did not understand that France's war in Cameroon was aimed no longer at preventing independence per se but at imposing another form of domination – behind the mask of nominal independence.

The UPC was not much listened to in Geneva or New York and was poorly understood in Paris and London. But it received firmer support in Accra and Conakry, the capitals of newly independent Ghana and Guinea. Félix Moumié was invited to the Ghanaian capital twice in 1958, for the First Conference of Independent African States in April and the All-African People's Conference in December. France had worked hard behind the scenes to encourage Ghanaian leader Kwamé Nkrumah to suspend the UPC president's invitation. Yet not only was Moumié welcomed, he was appointed to the conference steering committee. Worse still for the French authorities, the countries and organisations in attendance adopted a resolution demanding a total amnesty for UPC members, the return of political exiles, a referendum on the reunification of Cameroon and democratic elections under UN supervision.[10] For French officials, who were now doing everything in their power to 'secure' Cameroon's independence process, such a vote seemed like a dangerous prospect.

March 1959: the decisive battle at the UN

As we have said, Paris wanted to make the pseudo-independence granted to Cameroon an example for other territories in French-ruled Africa. This was just what it tried to do at the special session of the

UN General Assembly in New York from 20 February to 13 March 1959, at which France presented its plan for the lifting of its trusteeship over Cameroon.

Here, the French and Cameroon-nationalist representatives clashed in full view of the representatives of the international community. Hiding behind its Cameroonian allies, who were there to praise French policy, Paris defended its plans for independence without a referendum or prior elections. Such elections, Ahidjo argued, would amount to an 'unconditional surrender by a legal government, which had the vast majority of the country behind it, to a minority which had described itself as illegal'.[11] The UPC instead challenged this government's legitimacy: there was nothing democratic about the Legislative Assembly, since it was the result of the rigged December 1956 election in which the nationalists had been barred from running (see Chapter Three). The UPC ridiculed the idea that voters should be deprived of their rights on the grounds that they already agreed with the plans drawn up by their Franco-Cameroonian masters. This debate was, more fundamentally, about the definition of independence itself: would independence be in the hands of Cameroon's rulers or its inhabitants?

At the UN, this alternative was short-circuited by Cold War battle-lines. The French exploited these divides to convince their Western allies that the UPC proposal would amount to handing Cameroon to the Communist camp. In mid-March 1959, the French authorities won this decisive battle at the UN: the pro-French resolutions, supported by the United States, crushed the pro-UPC ones tabled by the group of eight non-aligned countries (Ethiopia, Ghana, Liberia, Libya, Morocco, the United Arab Republic, Sudan and Tunisia).

For France, this was a total victory. By getting a vote to lift the trusteeship 'without preconditions', it pulled off a double coup: on 1 January 1960, it granted an independence that would free it from UN constraints and cast itself in the upstanding role of the generous decoloniser, while also maintaining its leverage over the Cameroonian people thanks to the agreements it had got Ahidjo to sign. 'There is now a danger even more threatening than colonialism itself,' noted the Guinean representative to the UN. 'It is the danger that could be called a conceded independence, which tends to reflect the colonial power's own desires and tendencies within the country in question.'[12]

The propaganda noise around the UPC's alleged Communism thus played a decisive role in the nationalist party's defeat. Yet it is far from obvious that it had any such orientation. The UN vote proved it: while many Latin American and Asian states abstained because of the Communist label attached to the UPC leaders, the Communist bloc itself only weakly supported the Cameroonian nationalists. Having voted in vain against the pro-French resolutions during the preparatory vote in the Trusteeship Committee, the Eastern Bloc countries abstained the next day during the final vote in the General Assembly. Although there were individual UPC leaders who had some sympathy for Communism seen as a movement for human liberation, they had no steady strategic anchoring in the Communist camp.

When it came to building diplomatic relationships, the exiled UPC, which from 1957 to 1959 was mainly wrapped up in the pan-African struggle, was caught in a vice: it was too Communist for some but not Communist enough for others. This vote marked the end of the UPC's illusions about the UN process. Far from being a forum for international law, the UN was essentially a reflection of the balance between the great powers – especially as the non-aligned states, before the wave of independence declarations that came in 1960, were still very much in the minority.

In a kind of self-fulfilling prophecy, the UN decision tended to harden the UPC leadership's Communist image. Moumié and his comrades were well aware that they needed more powerful supporters. In the months that followed the UN vote, they thus stepped up their use of Marxist reference points in order to win the attention of potential

Communist allies, even at the cost of making their prose rather more leaden. It was, moreover, only after the UPC's defeat in New York that they began to receive – albeit weak – support from Moscow and Beijing. But the exiles still largely pinned their hopes on their African allies. Even while maintaining a Cairo office, the BCD decided to relocate to Conakry, where Moumié himself moved to, and to Accra, where a pan-African solidarity centre had been set up by the Ghanaian regime to take in representatives of the continent's liberation movements. This African Affairs Centre provided a means for the fighters still active on Cameroonian soil – who could take advantage of porous borders and also rely on the UPC's English-speaking allies, still active in the British zone – to keep in touch with exiles, either in person or via liaisons. It was also from here that dozens of fighters were soon sent off for political or military training in Morocco, Algeria, Egypt, the USSR and China.

May 1959: the ALNK at war with silence

After the clashes from the UN rostrum, the confrontation again returned to Cameroonian soil. The UPC leadership refused to give up despite the defeat just suffered in New York, and instead tried to intensify the struggle. It hoped that this could provoke a major crisis, which it saw as its only hope for placing Cameroon's fate back on the international agenda. Strongly backed up by France and sure of its own final victory, the Ahidjo government rejected the mediation proposals raised by Sékou Touré and Kwamé Nkrumah. 'The time has come', Ahidjo declared, 'to punish without mercy those who persist in perpetrating crimes against their compatriots and against the nation itself.'[13]

To break the silence that fell over Cameroon after the UN vote, the UPC steering committee set up a new armed organisation at the end of May 1959: the Kamerun National Liberation Army (ALNK), with

Martin Singap, a UPC militant who had distinguished himself in the ranks of the SDNK since 1957 (see Chapter Three), as chief of staff. Working directly with his comrades in Accra and Conakry, he managed to restructure the UPC military organisation, which had fallen into some disrepair. While the CNO had largely disintegrated in Sanaga-Maritime after Um Nyobè's death, it was in the Bamileke region, in the Mungo and in the Wouri that the new UPC military organisation was quickest to take shape.

Inspired by Algerian and Chinese methods, the ALNK's strategy was more radical than its predecessors' had been. Following the tried-and-tested technique of Algeria's National Liberation Army (ALN), the military wing of the FLN, the explicit aim now was to attack colonial interests and French nationals directly, violently and on a massive scale. From early summer 1959, there were rising numbers of raids in Yaoundé, Douala, Mungo and the Bamileke region carried out by groups or units of dozens of young men armed with machetes and clubs. Gendarmerie barracks, European plantations, Catholic missions and colonists' favoured hangouts (bars, cinemas, dance halls) were targeted, and several people killed. This offensive, which also allowed the ALNK to lay its hands on the weapons it so desperately lacked, sent the seventeen thousand French nationals living in Cameroon into psychosis.

These armed groups also attacked what they called the 'black colonists', meaning the Cameroonians who had sided with the French. There were mounting attacks on these 'lackeys', including former UPC activists who had recently rallied to the Ahidjo regime. These also served as warnings to the population. Using a mix of force and fear, the fighters stopped Cameroonians from collaborating with the authorities, obtained food supplies from local people, and 'recruited' fighters, nurses and cooks and took them off to the maquis. But intimidation was not always necessary; a French army intelligence bulletin in June 1959 reported: the 'vast majority of the population' considered the UPC 'a blessing'.[14] Indeed, the taxes demanded by the authorities were hard to come by: for they were instead funding the 'revolutionary struggle'.

The ALNK's success was all the more obvious because French leaders were so caught off guard. While aware that their opponents would not react passively to their defeat at the UN, they had not expected to be confronted this quickly with a massive, coordinated offensive. The economic warfare urged by Moumié turned out to be surprisingly effective: within a few months, banana and coffee production collapsed, putting European producers in serious trouble. As atrocities were reported from all over the territory and the bombing campaign gained momentum, French political and military leaders panicked.

The French were especially frustrated because the institutional situation of the autonomous State of Cameroon – a transitional status, prior to independence – put them in an uncomfortable position. While the agreements with Ahidjo had in many ways limited Cameroonian sovereignty, his government was still officially responsible for the difficult task of maintaining public order. Cameroon, it was explained, was soon to be independent and had to be able to manage its own affairs. But the autonomous state, which did not yet have its own armed forces, remained totally dependent on France for its security. The French strategy therefore consisted of putting Ahidjo front and centre and using his government as a façade for the campaign of repression. The French had to act behind the scenes.

A 'camouflaged system' of repression

More than ever surrounded by a hive of French advisers, the Cameroonian prime minister built up the young state's security arsenal. No punches were pulled. Even before the ALNK launched its offensive, Ahidjo took a series of extreme repressive measures to pre-emptively silence anyone who might wish to 'compromise public order'. In this vein, publications were subject to advance censorship, meetings and public gatherings were banned, passes were introduced to control and restrict freedom of movement, the periods of detainment without charge were arbitrarily extended, and special criminal courts with very broad jurisdiction were set up. To cap it all, a 'state of alert' was introduced across the whole southern part of the country. The rule of law to which Ahidjo had committed at the UN rostrum was reduced to nil.

While these measures were being enacted, in summer 1959 the French military organised a crackdown on the ALNK and its alleged supporters. But once again the French had to act discreetly, using the forces theoretically under Cameroonian government control as a 'camouflage'. The word was actually used in (or, rather, on) a document authored by the military commander of the French Forces in Cameroon. In line with the established agreements, he spoke of a 'permanent coordination' between the French and Cameroonians. But his superior, General Louis Le Puloch – commander of the AEF-Cameroun military zone (Zone d'outre-mer no. 2) – angrily corrected him with a note in the margin: this was 'not "coordination" but a *camouflaged system* [Le Puloch's emphasis] of command'.[15] The French military hierarchy thus showed the greatest discretion as it brought in seven additional infantry companies and ten gendarmerie platoons from French Equatorial Africa between July and October 1959.

Even more so than in the Sanaga-Maritime region during the period of the ZOPAC, the French army relied on the civilian population to punish the insurgents. Loudspeakers were loaded onto lorries and paraded around the Bamileke region to enlist the population. Tired of depending on hesitant or fickle local chiefs, French officials enrolled thousands of villagers and placed these militias under their own direct control, the better to comb the fields and mountains said to be 'infested' with rebels. 'A partisan every five metres and a soldier every forty-five metres,' one officer ordered during one of these operations, which in September 1959 mobilised some 13,000 people.[16] One military intelligence bulletin lauded militias 'driven by the desire to destroy and kill everything in their path'.[17] Terror spread throughout the Bamileke region. Villages were sealed off, hundreds of huts burnt down and women raped. Suspects were systematically tortured. In the big cities, particularly Douala, raids became a daily occurrence. Implementing the proposals made in 1955 by the head of the Wouri region, Bassa and Bamileke 'subversives' were put on trains and forcibly pushed back to their regions of origin. Once they got there, they fed the ranks of the nationalist movement.

Armed with the newly established special criminal courts, the judicial machine went into overdrive. Hundreds of defendants were paraded, their faces swollen by the beatings, before French judges who sent them to the dungeon or to be shot. The authorities were experimenting with a new method for exerting their psychological grip on the population: public executions. On 10 July 1959, five important 'gang leaders', including Pierre Simo – the former head of the SDNK, who had been handed over by British authorities a few months previously – were shot in Bafoussam market square. The local inhabitants, mustered en masse by loudspeaker, were forced to march past the corpses. This technique, which jarred with the principle of 'camouflaged' repression, was then suspended. But the number of enforced disappearances increased: during the night, 'suspects' were thrown alive into the huge waterfalls of the Bamileke region (see Chapter Three above).

Such methods naturally had an impact on the population, who were forced to take sides: despite the intense psychological-warfare campaign, they retreated into silence – an inscrutable attitude which was all the more worrying for French officials because the enemy seemed so elusive. Peaceful peasants who tilled their fields during the day joined the rebel groups at night. Worse still, women and children took part in the struggle (see box): one day passing messages to the maquis, the next day gathering in market squares to harass the troops and police.

Cameroonian women in the war

History as traditionally written is often replete with male protagonists and leaves little room for women. Yet many – often unfairly overlooked – women were driving forces in the Cameroonian nationalist movement.[18] The UPC did involve marginalised social categories, with young people and women at the forefront. There was also a special Union of Cameroonian Women (UDEFEC), created in 1954 in reaction to the marginalisation of the women's committees within the UPC itself. UDEFEC did not define itself as a feminist movement but did help to challenge the subordinate positions generally assigned to women by colonial and traditional authorities.[19]

Often led by the wives of UPC leaders, such as Marthe Moumié and Marthe Ouandié, women nationalist activists made a major contribution to establishing the movement and communicating with the UN, to which they sent countless petitions. After the war broke out, women played a major role in the maquis and as a support base for the rebellion, supplying food, money and ammunition and passing on intelligence. Women UPC fighters sometimes clashed directly with the repressive forces. 'The opponent sometimes consists of crowds of women numbering in the thousands, particularly at the markets,' French officers observed.[20]

In 1959, one intelligence officer denounced the 'packs of women opposing the forces of law and order in large numbers' – and the crackdown was severe. In October that same year, faced with the eight hundred women who had gathered at the Bafoussam airfield, the head of the gendarmerie brigade opened fire and killed three women demonstrators, so that his Jeep could make its way forward undisturbed. As in most wars, women were also the victims of reprisals. They were the victims of attacks and rapes designed as punishments for the chieftaincies opposed to the regime, or tortured, as was the case with the hunt for Um Nyobè.

Some women worked to promote official propaganda as part of the psychological warfare waged by the Cameroonian government. In the 1960s, for example, the president's wife Germaine Ahidjo travelled around the country to call for 'a return to calm' – terming this 'the essential condition for development' – and to draw 'wayward' women back into the women's structures of the ruling party, such as the Women's Organisation of the Cameroon Union (OFUC) created in 1965. Another example was Julienne Keutcha, a member of the National Assembly from 1960 and wife of Secretary of State Jean Keutcha, who criss-crossed the Bamileke region to spread the regime's message.

Because it is rarely mentioned in archives and often under-estimated by historians, the essential role played by women during the Cameroon War remains poorly documented. This is surely the reason why writers today are attempting to give them back the place they deserve in this history, sometimes in novel-ised form.[21]

In their internal reports in summer and autumn 1959, French officers were alarmed to see whole areas, populated by tens and even hundreds of thousands of people, fall under the insurgents' control. On the maps regularly updated by the French high command, the rebel zones grew larger by the week; in the Bamileke and Mungo regions the French soon controlled only the roads and urban centres. Even in Sanaga-Maritime, which had been thoroughly 'mopped up' over the previous months, the maquis reappeared. In Conakry, in Accra and in his interviews with journalists, Moumié had little fear of exaggerating when he hailed the 'heroic struggle of the people of Cameroon' and denounced the 'genocide' perpetrated by 'Franco-Ahidjo fascism'.[22]

The façade of independence: 1 January 1960

The exiles were all the more tempted to describe Ahidjo as an African version of Marshal Pétain after the Legislative Assembly vote on 29 October 1959, which handed the prime minister full powers for six months. Hence just two months before the final proclamation of independence, Ahidjo was the sole master of the country. The representatives of the French state and the French advisers to the Cameroonian state had been freed from UN oversight in March 1959 and from all parliamentary control in October. They could now negotiate the new Franco-Cameroonian agreements that would take effect at the moment of independence, and do so both with impunity and in full friendship with the Cameroonian head of government. Even more restrictive than the agreements signed in December 1958, and again containing secret clauses, these accords enabled the French army to intervene more openly against the rebellion, while codifying even tighter limits on Cameroonian sovereignty.

At the very moment when these documents were being signed, the ALNK and its satellites launched a vast offensive, which would continue to grow in the days and weeks that followed. Calling on friendly nations to boycott the independence festivities, which were being prepared in Yaoundé in a climate of terror, in December 1959 the UPC's BDC warned African leaders:

African problems are today so interdependent that no African should be indifferent to events taking place in this or that territory across our continent. If the fascist experiment against which the people of Kamerun are fighting succeeds, those so interested will not refrain from extending its field of application.[23]

The call for a boycott was not heeded, and Ahidjo proclaimed Cameroon's independence on 1 January 1960 in front of an adulatory audience of foreign dignitaries. While the unrest continued even just a few hundred metres away, the UN secretary general, the American ambassador to the UN, dozens of African representatives and even a few Soviet emissaries applauded the Cameroonian prime minister's speech. 'We know that the independence we have just gained would be nothing but an illusion if we could not ensure it in everyday reality,' promised Ahidjo. 'We are determined to give it a real existence, more than just a façade.' He was reading out a text drafted for him by his French aide Paul Audat, a colonial administrator who had just been transferred to 'assistance' duties.

5

Total War (1960–61)

France has had to stick to a certain restraint in recent months, as demanded by the particular situation in Cameroon. The Cameroonian government now enjoys full sovereignty, and is thus in a position to take the necessary measures.

— Charles de Gaulle, letter to the (French) president of the Cameroonian Chamber of Agriculture, 17 December 1959

In this lay a great irony: Cameroon's independence liberated France. Now free from UN control, and thus from international oversight of its handling of Cameroon, Paris could act as it pleased in this former trusteeship territory. The country was henceforth under joint management: it worked in tandem with Ahidjo's government, which had both freed itself of all parliamentary accountability with the full-powers vote and given up whole swathes of Cameroon's sovereignty to the former colonial master. Hence Cameroon's independence was a mere sham: national and popular sovereignty had been reduced to shreds.

Over the months following the official independence ceremonies on 1 January 1960, the urgent concern was to suppress the rebellion that continued to spread in the south of the country. This fight was to be waged behind the façade of independent Cameroonian leadership, but with ten times the resources. For this was the first consequence of Cameroonian independence: to free up the French armed forces in their fight to crush the UPC. According to the official version, which was widely relayed in the Paris press, France intervened militarily 'at the request of the government of Cameroon', 'in accordance with the texts binding the two countries'. But behind this façade, it was indeed the highest French authorities who were managing Cameroon's affairs.

Now that this country was 'independent', the Cameroon brief might naturally have been entrusted to the Ministry of Foreign Affairs. But much to the surprise of its offices – and to the foreign minister Maurice Couve de Murville himself, who described the handling of this procedural issue as 'quite extraordinary' – in January 1960 it instead fell to the prime minister's office at the Hôtel Matignon.[1] Prime Minister Michel Debré was in the front line, assisted by his loyal right-hand man, Constantin Melnik, who liaised with the secret services. Since this brief involved the French army, Debré handled it together with the minister for the armed forces – from February 1960 none other than Pierre Messmer, the former high commissioner in Yaoundé – and was assisted by Jean Lamberton, another expert on Cameroon, who became head of his military cabinet. The whole process was supervised by the Élysée, where Jacques Foccart, the 'man in the shadows' of the Gaullist regime, reigned supreme.

January 1960: France launches the 'reconquest'

In his memoirs, Debré makes no secret of his intentions at the time:

> At the start of 1960, the whole of the Bamileke country was outside the Cameroonian authorities' control. Ahidjo asked me to keep the French administrators in place – so be it! But that first decision was insufficient. I decided to launch an outright reconquest.[2]

To this end, the prime minister's office called in a specialist in counter-subversive warfare, one General Max Briand, who had, according to one of his colleagues, distinguished himself by his 'most pronounced taste for pacification efforts' in Indochina. As head of operations, Briand oversaw two operational zones: the Southern Battle Group (GTS), based in Douala, covering the southern part of the Mungo, the Wouri and the Sanaga-Maritime regions; and the Northern Battle Group (GTN), based in Bafoussam, bringing together eleven infantry companies, fifteen gendarmerie platoons and forty-nine groups of auxiliary commandos, a total of 3,500 men, to tackle the most 'infested' areas: the northern part of the Mungo and the Bamileke *département*.

Commanded by French officers, these units were staffed by Africans, for reasons of saving money, discretion and 'efficiency'. The hundreds of soldiers sent from the countries of the French Community (the former AEF and AOF) were gradually joined by thousands of local militiamen, grouped together in what was known as the Civic Guard in the Bamileke region and the Free Corps in the Mungo region. In parallel to this a new stratagem, air raids, was deployed. From the airports at Douala and Koutaba (in the loyalist Bamoun *département*), planes – piloted by French nationals – were launched over the Bamileke region. Hundreds of rockets and tens of thousands of incendiary cartridges were dropped on the 'infected zones' over the following months, in addition to the countless combing and cordoning operations carried out on the ground: 'Alpha', 'Charlie', 'Épervier', 'Babouche', 'Martinet', 'Étincelle', 'ABC' and so on.

In March 1960, a *Le Figaro* journalist flew over the Bamileke region's Bamboutos mountains in a French army observation plane. He spoke of a landscape of chaos. 'Waves of flames gripped the fields . . . devouring everything that grew there,' he reported. 'I started to count how many houses were ablaze but stopped at fifty: what point could this have, when everything was burning along a valley twenty kilometres long?' There were 'hundreds of houses . . . skeletons of soot-black brick, without beams or rafters, without roofs

or doors, all enveloped in the hot smell of burning flesh'. If this oblig-
ing journalist was still keen on the French intervention, this was
because he had not the slightest doubt that the macabre scene must
have been created by terrorists who, he said, were 'dancing a wild jig
around the infernos'.[3]

The situation differed somewhat when seen from less lofty heights
(see box below). While we could cite many accounts, the testimony
of Cameroonian pastor Pierre Talla, written down by a European
colleague shortly after the events, is especially worth quoting. On 9
April 1960, when the rebels who had been occupying the Bangang
mission had left the premises, loyalist soldiers arrived in the village.
According to Talla,

> The soldiers were firing from all sides, the bullets were whistling over
> our heads. The planes never stopped machine-gunning; we didn't know
> what to do; the huts were burning everywhere; they were killing people.
> Pregnant women were disembowelled and children torn limb from
> limb; people were frightfully beheaded. This went on from seven in the
> morning until two in the afternoon.

Having escaped the carnage and 'stepped over countless corpses', he
came across a French soldier who was surprised to see him still alive.
The pastor was himself amazed that the villagers had been massacred
after the 'rebels' had already left. The Frenchman replied: 'That's true,
but there's nothing else to be done in such rotten corners.'[4]

Through this use of collective punishment, the French officers who
headed the operation sought to sow chaos in the rebels' ranks and cut
them off from the general population. And yet, supported by thousands of villagers who provided them with supplies and information,
the maquisards showed remarkable resilience. Over February 1960,
the ALNK managed to strike serious blows at their enemies, and
Martin Singap even managed to attack loyalist troops from the rear as

they ripped through the 'infested zones'. This was much to the dismay of Lieutenant-Colonel René Gribelin, commander of the Northern Battle Group and a veteran of Indochina who had encountered many such difficulties before. 'Sure of their strength, brave to the point of recklessness, driven by a blind faith in their sorcerers', he wrote, the rebels could rely on a powerful weapon: 'easy and almost unlimited recruitment'. He sullenly concluded: 'The adversary the GTN will be up against is not to be discounted.'[5]

The war seen from the ground

For many, the air raids launched by the French army at the beginning of 1960, which spread fire and bloodshed across West Cameroon, are still etched in the memory. Retired teacher Jean Donfack, a young maquisard at the time, told us in 2008: 'We used to hide under the rocks to see how they did it. There were two planes, always two planes.' Mimicking the planes that could fly 'in any position', he goes on to describe: 'The first one dropped petrol on the roofs. Then the second one would come down and shoot a red bullet at the same spot, and it would catch fire. That's how it always happened.'

Djumo Youmbi, who was twenty-one years old in February 1960, experienced his first air attacks just a few months after he joined the Accra maquis in West Cameroon. He told us in 2007: 'They came to bomb people in Bamena. Some were wounded. We were able to transport some of them into the town. Others died in my arms . . . They were so badly burnt . . . I didn't have enough stuff to treat them with.' Having rescued eight people in this situation, Youmbi remembers 'this kind of burn': 'It was as if they had been pushed into a big fire. It swelled them up. When it gets you in the stomach, in the back, you don't survive.'

Daniel Maugué, a Cameroonian journalist and editor of the Protestant weekly *La Semaine camerounaise*, told us in 2007 that these raids targeted all kinds of gathering indiscriminately:

> When it came to a funeral or a burial [and these were each banned], the soldiers did everything to disperse the crowds. When the army learnt that there was going to be a gathering, they organised to attack, often with bombs or grenades, and many people died. That's why people were so scared as soon as they heard the sound of an aeroplane. Everyone went and hid in some nook, under the trees, in the forest, in the shallows, in the swamps.

In early February 1960, Daniel Galland, a pastor from Dschang who was quite hostile to the UPC, wrote to the Protestant newspaper *Réforme* to protest against the increasingly violent repression:

> For three days now, the forces of order have been attacking the maquis. I don't know what will be left of certain villages, because the Cameroon government is determined to strike a blow, unfortunately with the help of the French army . . . The corpses are no longer even buried, there are just too many of them. When the maquisards are caught making trenches in the roads, they are killed with machine guns and buried with the earth collected by the bulldozers to fill the holes. In some places, pigs act as gravediggers . . . It's horrible. No more prisoners [are taken]. There is not even mercy for the women and children. Indeed, women are not the least savage in war.

But what horrified this witness most was the general feeling that a threshold of violence had been crossed in the minds of the belligerents: 'The gendarmes you hear in Dschang talk about these massacres in a perfectly natural tone. Human life no longer matters.'[6]

In 2008 we spoke to Jacques Mermier, a conscript who did his military service in Cameroon from May to July 1960. He confirmed the mindset of the career soldiers alongside whom he flew the planes that bombed the Bamileke region: 'They didn't ask themselves many questions; they just wanted to get a good write-up and make sure their aircraft didn't crash when they went into a dive. They'd strafe the villages without a second thought.'

But gradually the French forces gained the upper hand. Through several months of operations, they were able to gather strategic intelligence, infiltrate the enemy troops, turn important insurgents, cut off communications between leaders, recruit civic guards, and enrol a growing number of peasants in 'self-defence' units. Put to this severe test, Singap – the remarkably resilient ALNK leader – changed his strategy in summer 1960. He called on non-combatants, subject to indiscriminate repression and struggling to survive precarious illegal conditions, to return to legality while continuing to help the insurgents in secret. 'The enemies of our country will take you for defectors', he explained, 'but you will know what you are.'[7] In the weeks and months that followed, tens of thousands of people gradually returned to the French side.

These French forces shrank from no atrocity in the quest for such successes. In addition to bombings, arson attacks and indiscriminate massacres, torture was practised on a vast scale and public executions carried out before stunned crowds. The condemned rebels' bodies were left in full view of locals for weeks on end. Another technique used in this terror strategy was the display of severed heads. This terrifying exhibition of decapitated human beings in village squares and by the roadsides became so commonplace across the span of several years that the witnesses whom we interviewed almost half a century later sometimes forgot to mention this 'detail'. It was, however, a significant detail when we consider that the skulls of the dead hold a central place in the Bamileke belief system: sacred, they serve as intermediaries to address the Nsi, this monotheistic people's god.

The year 1960 was, then, a terrible one. While stressing that 'the figures are open to question', Max Briand drew up the following tally: 'The total losses of the Bamileke population in 1960 amounted to a little more than 20,000 men', including '5,000 killed in combat', '5,000 who fell victim to disease', '1,000 who died from their injuries' and '10,000' others killed in a mysterious 'internal struggle'. As if to offset this astronomical death toll, Briand immediately adds, 'This number should be compared to the estimated annual demographic growth, of between 22,000 and 25,000.'[8] In other words, seeing as births made up for deaths, there was no reason for outrage. In October 1962, *Le Monde*'s André Blanchet cited a different number:

> Someone, whose claims I have not been able to verify but whose allegations deserve to be taken seriously, told me that there had been a total of 120,000 victims during the two or three years that the insurrection lasted in the [Bamileke] country; but we were almost totally ignorant of this even in France, the former colonial homeland.[9]

The Bamileke people, a 'stone in the shoe'

Max Briand's reconquest operations took place in an almost total media blackout. Kept away from the theatres of operations, few international newspapers still took an interest in Cameroon, which had become a foreign country. The handful of journalists who paid attention to the unrest, and whose reporting itself took place under close military surveillance, never questioned the French authorities. They preferred to describe the conflict – in the manner of the *Figaro* journalist flying over the Bamboutos – as a 'mixture of banditry, tribal warfare, a return to nature, under the influence of the typical energies of eternal Africa'.[10] In short, they treated it as something irrational and apolitical – an attitude akin to Briand's own summary judgement, in describing the insurrection simply as 'illogical'.

The French leaders offered an equally perfunctory analysis of the situation. While making full use of the Communist scarecrow, they increasingly insisted on putting ethnicity at the heart of their rhetoric. After the Bassa, who had been so vilified at the time of the ZOPAC, the pacification zone, the Bamileke were now dragged over the coals. In March 1960, Colonel Lamberton wrote in the prestigious journal *Défense nationale*: 'Cameroon has embarked on the road to independence with a bothersome stone in its shoe.' But what was this stone? 'The presence of an ethnic minority: the Bamileke, in the grip of convulsions whose origins and causes are not clear to anyone.' Describing this 'people alien to Cameroon' as an existential threat – a 'homogeneous group of Negro populations' said to have 'spread' into the Mungo before 'invading' other regions, to the point of making Douala 'practically a Bamileke town' – this ethnically charged text reads like the vade-mecum of the French soldiers mobilised in Cameroon.[11] It is today often cited as evidence by those who denounce a French 'genocide' in Cameroon, pointing to the staggering human toll of repression.

Rather than being genocidal in intent, in the strict sense, for the French, the war was primarily aimed at subduing and disciplining unruly populations through a 'reconquest' of their territory – but also of their minds. The aim was to keep the population under control, within the framework of a nation that was itself strictly controlled by the neocolonial pact. Indeed, the military operations launched in 1960 aimed not just at suppressing the enemy but at completely reorganising the targeted societies, which were considered universally suspect. As the troops advanced across the terrain, the politico-military authorities confined the populations that had been 'won over' in resettlement camps created from scratch. These facilities were surrounded by barbed wire, guarded by watchtowers, and controlled by civic guards and self-defence units. The policy of 'villagisation', tried out in other colonial areas and implemented in the Sanaga-Maritime region between 1957 and 1958, was reproduced in the Bamileke region in the 1960s.

The civic guards played a central role in this apparatus of Cameroonian political and military self-control. These local auxiliaries, which were officially formed by the French authorities at the beginning of 1960, were not only used to fight the insurgents directly. They were also given a psychological mission: to monitor and (re-)educate the people who had come back under their authority, whether they were willing or not. This psychological-warfare effort, which took the form of training sessions, 'detoxification' sessions and film screenings, intensified as the months went by. Given the 'hypocrisy of the Bamileke element', as the head of Cameroon's intelligence service put it, the resettlement camps were designed to 'psychologically correct' and 'morally rearm' the Bamileke population.[12]

Hence alongside the more properly military campaign, a new political and social order was being established in the region. Characterised by sparse settlements and pretty thatched roofs, the rolling hills of this region, often described as the 'Auvergne of Africa', were transformed into a field of ruins and militarised camps. 'The Bamileke landscape has been utterly transformed, with the scattered family concessions having disappeared along with the traditional hut to make way for large villages,' wrote the French ambassador to Prime Minister Debré in November 1960 after visiting the resettlement camps alongside Briand. Welcoming the 'relaxed, even smiling attitude of the inhabitants' in these fortified villages, the authorities continued apace with the resettlement policy.[13] Two years into the 'reconquest', no fewer than 462,000 people were parked in these camps in the Bamileke region, according to the figures the ambassador provided to Jacques Foccart.[14]

Vilifying the Bamileke people in this way, the authorities were not only pursuing a policy of exception in this one region – enlisting the 'loyal' masses to eliminate 'terrorists' and eradicate subversive ideas – for this also encouraged the other 'ethnicities' to repel the threat posed by this new enemy within. As early as January 1960, friendly forces began attacking the Bamileke. Hence on 24 January that year the ultra-loyalist Bamoun sultan and three thousand of his men launched reprisals against the Bamileke village of Bamendjin and the Bamileke inhabitants of the town of Foumbot. When the gendarmerie saw the devastation, they reported 'many dead', with their decapitated heads reportedly taken to the sultan. Something similar happened on 24 April in the Congo district of Douala, where the Haoussa people, originally from the north, had – as a *Figaro* journalist put it three months earlier – formed a 'first-rate phalanx in the hierarchy of counter-revolution'.[15] At a time when attacks by the ALNK were mounting in the city, some Haoussa reportedly set fire to the neighbourhood, which was mainly populated by Bamileke. Official figures put the death toll at nineteen, with one thousand huts destroyed and five thousand people left homeless. While imprecise, the unofficial figures point to much higher numbers and contradict Briand's internal reports when they claim that these events had a 'distinctly tribal character'. Some sources even claim that the army had surrounded the neighbourhood, under the watchful eye of a helicopter, and had opened fire on those who desperately tried to escape the flames.

The security backbone of the Yaoundé regime

The new Cameroonian state had been born in a warlike atmosphere; and it was now transformed into a counter-subversive machine, under the pseudo-democratic trappings of a façade of sovereignty. When French officials gave way to Cameroonians, this was lauded by foreign observers, who welcomed the 'Cameroonisation' of the state administration. And yet real power still eluded the native population. The French, who had become a cooperating power, remained omnipresent behind the scenes and often dictated their laws to their new supposed bosses. At the same time, the new Cameroonian officials' prerogatives were discreetly transferred to higher-level authorities – with the effect that their new functions were, if surely gratifying, little more than honorary positions.

At the moment of independence, only a few Cameroonians had any influence. One of these was Samuel Kamé. Cunning, ultra-authoritarian and an unconditional follower of counter-subversive methods, from 1957 onwards he played a key role, alongside Maurice Delauney, in the suppression of the insurrection in the Bamileke region (see Chapter Three). He continued to follow this brief very closely even thereafter, often in a covert manner. One of the few Cameroonians who enjoyed the confidence of Ahidjo, who was in general rather suspicious of his compatriots, Kamé held several discreet but strategic positions. During this period, he became the éminence grise of the emerging regime, though the French ambassador noted that Kamé 'made no secret of his preference for a fascist-style policy'.[16]

The spirit that inspired the drafting of the independent state's Constitution in early 1960 offers a perfect illustration of how Cameroonisation served as an optical illusion. Drawn up by two of the 'cooperating' French officials, Paul Audat and Jacques Rousseau, the constitutional text was discussed by a commission from the Cameroonian Assembly. But the decisions were actually taken out of sight, in the presence of Ahidjo, Kamé and their French advisers. In his memoirs, Jacques Rousseau relates his discussions with Kamé in this small committee: 'As you see it Samuel, the Constitution should stop at just three articles: 1) the President of the Republic is called Ahmadou Ahidjo; 2) he holds all the powers of the Republic; 3) he exercises them for life.' And he added: 'In reality, I was not far from seeing things as Kamé did, but I thought it advisable to dress up such an abrupt text in the appropriate manner.'[17] But what did 'dressing it up' mean? The aim was to give the new Constitution the same look and feel as the French Fifth Republic's – a democratic appearance, with a prime minister and an assembly – but above all to make sure to preserve Article 16 of the French Constitution (which was Article 20 in the Cameroonian text) allowing the president to assume full powers in an emergency.

This Constitution came into force after a rigged referendum held on 20 February 1960: the figures were fixed in the south, which overwhelmingly rejected the document, and inflated in the north, which had a thin majority in favour. The same masquerade was repeated for the parliamentary elections on 10 April, which handed most seats to Ahidjo's Cameroonian Union. The new Assembly appointed Ahidjo, who was the only candidate, to the post of president of the Republic. He then immediately issued a decree instituting a state of emergency in eleven of the country's twenty-three *départements*. Civil liberties were restricted and the military courts given broader jurisdiction. The French authorities noted the benefits of the 'negotiated independence' rubber-stamped by the UN in 1959: unlike in Togo, where referendums and elections, supervised by the United Nations, had brought the nationalist Sylvanus Olympio to power in 1958 (see Chapter Four above), the ballots organised in a vacuum in Cameroon two years later made it possible, in the words of a letter written in January 1960 and found in Jacques Foccart's archives, 'to entrust quasi-dictatorial power to the man trusted by a certain France'.[18]

The repressive apparatus took form in parallel to the creation of Cameroon's other new institutions. Officially founded in November 1959, the army was the backbone of the new regime. But during the first years of independence, it remained in French hands, thanks to the military cooperation agreements signed between Ahidjo and the former colonial power. Not until 1965 would a Cameroonian, General Pierre Semengue, become head of the army proper, and only in 1966 did the gendarmerie come under Cameroonian command (the air force remained in French hands later still). It should also be pointed out that all Cameroonian military personnel were trained – and equipped – by the French and that, given the circumstances, the doctrine of revolutionary war served as the core of this training. Colonel Lacheroy's theories and the lessons of the Battle of Algiers became the gospel for the new recruits.

The first director of Cameroon's Combined Arms Military School (EMIA) in 1960 was a French officer, Jacques-Louis Lefevre, who had served under Bigeard in Indochina and Algeria, where he was accused of torturing prisoners, before being sent to fight against the insurgents in the Mungo region. The students in the EMIA's inaugural levy, which was christened 'Independence', remembered him as a brutal man who beat up young soldiers and had a taste for torture. Colonel Paul-Théodore Ndjock, a graduate of this class at the school, told us in 2008: 'Of course, they didn't teach us how to use the *gégène* [electric generator for torture] in the lectures at the EMIA. But we were shown it during a course at Yaoundé central prison, with the magneto attached to the genitals.'[19] Colonel Sylvestre Mang, from the same year group, confirms: 'A para can only give a para-commando flavour to young people,' he explains. '[Lefevre] wanted fighters. With him the mood was Indochina, it was Algeria . . . All the instructors were like that. Even when we had independence, they still wanted to fight the war. They were trained for that; they grew up with this mentality. It made them, and they ended up making it a way of life, a religion.'[20] Lefevre left Cameroon in 1962 – to join the OAS, according to some accounts – and he was replaced at the head of the EMIA by other Frenchmen, up till 1986.

Although from 1960 the minister of armed forces was a Cameroonian, the ministry's real boss was another Frenchman, Colonel Jean-Victor Blanc, who from October 1960 to 1966 held the dual post of chief of staff of the Cameroonian Army and head of the armed forces section of the French military mission. General Semengue, who knew him well, described him as an exceptional man of remarkable discretion. While on paper he was a mere technical adviser to the Ministry of Armed Forces, in reality his influence spread far and wide: 'He wrote the minister's notes to the president . . . and the president's reply to the minister! So, in fact, he was everything. But he did not *seem* to be everything.' Colonel Blanc's discretion is a perfect illustration of the pretence of a false independence. He soon became one of the president's most trusted confidants, as Ahidjo appreciated both his effective work and his discretion; but he was also making regular reports to the French embassy, the authority to which he really answered.[21] The French ambassador Francis Huré, who was posted to Cameroon from 1965 to 1968, told us, '[Blanc] was supposed to obey only Ahidjo. But it was almost a joke. In reality, Blanc answered to Renan [military counsellor at the French embassy], and Renan asked me what he had to do.'[22]

This double hierarchy, maintained over some years, can be seen throughout the entire security apparatus of the Cameroonian state, of which it formed the backbone.[23] The police and intelligence services were likewise staffed by Cameroonians trained in France itself and by French advisers who, as well as helping their local counterparts to set up 'effective' services, monitored them on behalf of their superiors in Yaoundé and, more often still, in Paris. One part of this security architecture especially worth mentioning was a low-profile body created by the colonial administration even before independence: the Studies and Documentation Bureau (BEDOC), formally established in March 1960 and renamed the Studies and Documentation Service (SEDOC) the following year. An outright political police force, it oversaw a joint civilian-military body, the Mixed Mobile Brigades (BMM), made up of French and Cameroonian gendarmes, police and military personnel. The BMM made especially boundless use of violence and torture. Here again, we see this same 'doubling up': attached directly to the Cameroonian presidency, SEDOC had an almost organic link with the French intelligence services to the extent that this structure – described as one of the 'most effective political police forces in Black Africa' – was long regarded as nothing more than the local branch of the French External Documentation and Counter-Espionage Service (SDECE).

November 1960: the assassination of Félix Moumié and the signing of the neocolonial pact

The French intelligence services left no stone unturned during this postindependence period. Well aware that threats to Cameroon were not confined to its borders, they also tracked down the 'Communist' exiles active abroad. Their main target, of course, was Félix Moumié.

The UPC president was a passionate, tenacious figure, and after the defeat at the UN in 1959 he worked hard to find diplomatic, financial and material support for the ALNK fighters. Already close to the Ghanaian and Guinean governments, he built ties with the rising figure of African nationalism, Congo's Patrice Lumumba, whom he met in Accra in April 1960. Six months later, Moumié flew to the newly independent Congo to set up a UPC base there. But he arrived in Léopoldville at the worst possible moment: Lumumba had been taken captive by forces loyal to Colonel Joseph-Désiré Mobutu, the country's new Western-backed strongman, who immediately expelled the Cameroonian nationalist leader to Accra. From there, the indefatigable Moumié set off without delay for his final destination: Geneva.

The French services were on the UPC leader's trail and had come up with an elaborate plan to eliminate him. Some time after making contact with Moumié in Accra, a fake Geneva-based journalist – who was in fact working for the SDECE – took advantage of Moumié's visit to Switzerland to invite him to dinner in a restaurant in the Swiss city on 13 October 1960. As Moumié got up to take a telephone call from an SDECE accomplice, the agent poured thallium into the glass of his target – who did not drink it – and then into a second glass. But finally, Moumié gulped down both glasses in one go, imbibing a larger-than-intended dose of the poison, which was supposed to work slowly in order to cover the agent's tracks. The UPC president, himself a medical doctor, thus had the time to name his assassin before he lost consciousness. The SDECE agent, William Bechtel, promptly disappeared, leaving the Swiss police to find damning evidence in his home.

Unlike the French media, which quickly buried the affair, Swiss television interviewed Ernest Ouandié, vice-president of the UPC, and Félix Moumié's widow, who had each urgently come to Switzerland upon his passing on 3 November 1960. Both they and their interviewer made clear where responsibility lay. All signs pointed to the Red Hand, a murky organisation which – it was discovered at the time – was secretly used by the French secret services to liquidate those who got in the way of its African policy, particularly in Algeria.

[The Red Hand] is an organisation that reports directly to the French *deuxième bureau* [the historic name for foreign military intelligence], which operates not only in your country but in Belgium, West Germany and Italy and has already claimed many victims in African-nationalist circles,

Ouandié explained to the Swiss television channel RTS. 'Last year, I was in London on my way to the United Nations, where I was to be heard as a petitioner, and I was there with the president of our party, who was headed on a mission to Europe. He had been threatened by an agent who clearly told him that he was a member of the Red Hand.'[24] It would be years before these accusations, which eventually were substantiated, were accurately documented and acknowledged by the top leadership of the French secret services.

On 13 November 1960, ten days after Moumié's death, the bilateral agreements governing Franco-Cameroonian relations, which until then had been provisional, were finally set in stone. Close to a dozen agreements and conventions severely restricted Cameroon's sovereignty in the military, economic, monetary, diplomatic, cultural and judicial domains. These accords ensured that thousands of French 'technical assistants' would remain on Cameroonian soil, and the military agreements also kept French boots on the ground. As for the highly sensitive defence agreements signed on the same day, they have never been revealed (even after they were revised in the 1970s and again in 2009). The UPC, preoccupied by the mysterious Moumié affair, barely reacted. Hence the colonial pact which definitively bound Cameroon to France was signed amid almost total silence.

The annexation of West Cameroon

While the Bamileke people were described as an enemy within – and some of Cameroon's leaders even started to believe it – French officials were more worried about their real adversaries: their geopolitical rivals. Of course, these included the Communist powers, suspected of trying to gain a foothold in decolonised Africa. But beyond the anti-Bamileke and anti-Communist propaganda, the French had other, less official rivals: the British, historical competitors of French power on the continent, and, behind them, the Americans, whom the Gaullist regime saw with some suspicion. This more global geostrategic game is an important dimension of any analysis of the conflict in Cameroon.

Cameroon's history and geographical position ensured its place at the heart of these contests. A study of the British and French archives from this period clearly shows that when it came to Cameroonian issues, relations between London and Paris were far from serene. The British were suspicious of France, which claimed to be decolonising without actually doing so, and was constantly trying to impose its agenda on them. The French, meanwhile, were continually riled by the alleged laxity of the British, who stood accused of allowing ALNK 'terrorists' a free hand to use the British zone as a rear base from which to launch their offensives in the Mungo and Bamileke regions. In Paris it was believed that this soft-touch approach betrayed a British interest in dominating the continent economically, a plan which also involved integrating the Cameroons into the vast Nigerian state, just as they had driven the swallowing up of former British Togo by Ghana. At times, French suspicions bordered on paranoia, forcing the British to repeat to their French counterparts that they did not 'direct' Kwamé Nkrumah any more than the Americans controlled Sékou Touré's Guinea.

While the British authorities stepped up their surveillance of UPC circles in the territory they controlled, Franco-British tensions were still high when voters in the British Cameroons went to the polls on 11 February 1961 to choose their future path. Two separate referendums were held that day, with two opposed results. With the option of full independence effectively off the ballot, voters in the Northern Cameroons opted to join Nigeria (which had become independent on 1 October 1960), while those in the Southern Cameroons opted to become part of the former French Cameroon (which it was to join on 1 October 1961).

For the young Cameroonian government, in need of at least the veneer of nationalist legitimacy, the battle over reunification was a godsend. After championing the idea of an 'independent and reunified' Cameroon during the referendum campaign, Ahidjo and his cronies cried foul over the rigging of the election results in the Northern Cameroons. The government declared a day of national mourning and lodged an appeal with international bodies, albeit without success. It has to be said that this partial reunification put the regime in Yaoundé in a tricky position: it meant a merger with the 800,000 inhabitants of the Southern Cameroons, assimilated to the Bamileke people with whom they shared a border, without this being offset by the inhabitants

of the Northern Cameroons, who were of a similar number but per-
ceived as naturally loyal to the Cameroonian president, who also hailed
from the north of the country. But Ahidjo quickly made up for lost
time: he imposed on his new English-speaking compatriots a purportedly federal Constitution, which would in theory give a say to the
representatives of the former British Southern Cameroons (renamed
West Cameroon); but real power lay solely with the federal president
himself. Officially absent from the negotiations, the French once again
played an important behind-the-scenes role in orchestrating this sleight
of hand. In 2008, Ahidjo's legal adviser, Jacques Rousseau, told us
how his colleagues had tricked the other side in the talks: 'I had drawn
up a vicious little thing, with a federal president who would hold all the
power.' For Rousseau, 'in these countries, one potentate is better than
several: an enlightened despotism, as it were'.[25] Taken over by Franco-
Cameroonian military forces on 1 October 1961, the English-speaking
region of reunified Cameroon immediately understood how enlightened this despotism really was (see box below).

'French control' of Cameroon as seen by the British in 1963

The French have, with remarkable success, exorcised the nation-
alistic spirit by granting political independence, while hanging on
to all the controlling strings. Political decisions, though taken by
Cameroonians, cannot help reflecting the still almost complete
economic, financial, commercial, cultural and military dependence on France.

This implacable denunciation of French neocolonialism in Cameroon does not come from a leaflet by opponents in exile but
from a confidential report by the British embassy in Cameroon,
dated 26 April 1963.[26]

'French influence behind the scenes is powerful,' it explains. First of all, 'French military assistance is indispensable'. 'The Cameroon army and gendarmerie are both commanded by French colonels and contain over 200 French officers and NCOs. In addition, there are over 1000 men of the French army in Cameroon.' In the event of danger, 'the Head of the French Military Mission is empowered under a Franco-Cameroonian military agreement to take command of all the French and Cameroonian forces in the country'.

The report depicts an economy entirely in the hands of its former colonial master. 'If the French were to pull out overnight, therefore, commercial life in East Cameroon would virtually cease to exist.' This was shown by Cameroon's dependence on France for its foreign trade: 'France supplies 58% of East Cameroonian imports and takes 62% of her exports.' In the end, 'France puts a lot of money into Cameroon and takes a lot out . . . but it is probable that she still makes an overall "profit"'.

This was also a cultural stranglehold insofar as most of Cameroon's elites, educated in France, were, 'in effect, Frenchmen with black skins'. The *brevet* and *baccalauréat* examinations were 'set and corrected in France' to the point that Cameroonian students were asked to 'describe the spring' in a tropical country that has no such season.

For the report's author, the imposition of such a centralised, authoritarian, unequal model, ultimately cut off from Cameroonian realities, presented 'long-term political risks'. The report especially noted that this stemmed from the 'creation of a highly-paid class of politicians and "fonctionnaires" who live far above and largely out of touch with the majority of the population'.

Spreading the 'Cameroon model'

At the end of 1961, the French could count themselves lucky. Despite – or rather thanks to – a particularly difficult situation, owing to Cameroon's legal status and the ALNK uprising, they had managed to keep the country, now enlarged by some 45,000 square kilometres, within France's orbit. How? Firstly, by making the leader whom they had installed sign Cameroon up to permanent agreements that drastically restricted its national sovereignty. Secondly, by launching a brutal wave of repression that severely curtailed any real democratic life. The three-year transition period from 1959 to 1961 had, of course, resulted in tens of thousands of deaths. But the political outcome was so satisfactory for France that Cameroon looked like a model to follow elsewhere in Africa.

Examining the French political, diplomatic and military archives from the transition period, we find that this rather particular country, which had once been considered a breach in the imperial edifice, was now described as an example. True, Cameroon's leaders managed to avoid integration into the Fifth Republic's French Community (a move which would have risked repelling voters in the referendums in the British Cameroons). But in a moment when the former African colonies were one by one gaining independence in 1960, and as the ill-conceived French Community splintered in the months that followed, France's relations with these new nations followed in Cameroon's footsteps. Their armies were built on the same counter-subversive model. Their secret services were trained at the same school and organically bound to their French counterparts. Their pro-French leaders in turn became apprentice dictators, backed up by similar constitutions inspired by the Fifth Republic's own, and closely monitored by Liaison and Intelligence Posts (PLR) with which the SDECE locked down France's African backyard. All these leaders signed bilateral agreements, similar to the ones signed by Ahidjo in 1958, which placed draconian limits on their sovereignty. Those who refused faced merciless resistance, as in the case of Sékou Touré in Guinea, or physical elimination, like Togo's Sylvanus Olympio (assassinated in 1963).

The first in a long list of neocolonial wars launched by Paris in defence of its interests, France's military intervention in Cameroon in 1960 also set a precedent: French leaders would have no hesitation in directly intervening in the independent states of French-speaking Africa. The same methods were used each time: a call for help from a puppet president in dire straits, an operation camouflaged by skilful propaganda, cutting-edge weapons in support of local auxiliary units, direction from the French president without any accountability to parliament.

Of course, Cameroon was not the only model: Françafrique was also invented in parallel in the Gabon of Léon Mba and Omar Bongo and in the Côte d'Ivoire of Félix Houphouët-Boigny. But plenty of archival sources show that the Cameroonian experience frequently served as a benchmark and as an inspiration. The men who had suppressed the UPC and installed the Ahidjo regime between 1957 and 1961 profited greatly from their experience in Cameroon later in their careers in other African countries where they offered their cooperation. Such was the case of the police official Georges Conan, who was in charge of intelligence in the Sanaga-Maritime, Mungo and Bamileke regions between 1957 and 1959 and then 'director of interrogations' at the BMM. He went on to head the Gabonese political police, under the leadership of former Bamileke regional head Maurice Delauney, who became French ambassador to Libreville and was in direct contact with Jacques Foccart. We could likewise mention the case of Daniel Doustin, a theorist of Cameroonian-style neocolonialism, who became head of France's Directorate of Territorial Surveillance (DST) in the 1960s and chief of staff to Prime Minister Raymond

Barre in the 1970s. And of course there was Pierre Messmer, who along with Colonel Lamberton moved from the High Commissariat for Cameroon to the Ministry of the Armed Forces before being named prime minister by Georges Pompidou in 1972.

The shift from a colonial logic to a neocolonial frame was accompanied by a change in the French governmental set-up: African affairs, which had been jointly managed by different ministries before 1961–62, came under the increasingly tight control of the president. It was from the Élysée Palace that Foccart – de Gaulle's Africa adviser and the lynchpin of all manner of sinister networks – steered France's Africa policy and the activities of its secret services, not hesitating to enmesh them in his own webs of connections. This increasingly secretive and personalised approach, which benefited from the departure of Michel Debré – and Constantin Melnik, Foccart's great rival – in April 1962, enabled this shadowy figure to forge closer links with the African leaders, who were themselves increasingly despotic. Digging through Foccart's archives, which are now available to researchers, we can only be astonished by the number – and sometimes the triviality – of requests that African leaders addressed to him. They might plead one day for an extension of credit or the closer surveillance of an opponent and the next day beg for a place for their son in a French university or – like Ahidjo in October 1962 – a signed photo of General de Gaulle.

This is what created the order today known as Françafrique. It is a unique system of neocolonial governance that enables a tiny number of French officials, in collusion with a handful of African leaders, to control remotely and at low cost what the theorist of counter-subversive strategy Charles Lacheroy described in his memoirs as 'tadpole states'. By this he meant states with a big head, the well-stuffed ruling class, and a small body, the 'underdeveloped' peoples who remain prisoners of a system that ensures their continued domination by the old colonial power.

6

Administering Terror

In a situation like ours, [we must] organise militias made up of young people of both sexes. Do not hesitate to imitate fascist methods: squads, sections, companies, battalions, regiments, divisions (Germany).
—Samuel Kamé, 'L'UC doit-elle être un parti de masse ou un parti d'élites?', August 1961

While the assassinations of both Ruben Um Nyobè and Félix Moumié in the space of just two years had dramatically weakened the UPC, the Franco-Cameroonian authorities nevertheless kept up their offensive throughout the 1960s. This military campaign was no longer directed solely against the armed rebellion, which continued despite fierce repression, or even against the populations suspected of supporting it, particularly in the Bamileke region. Rather, the counter-subversive warfare which had been conceived in the late 1950s as a temporary measure was now generalised, institutionalised and turned into the routine reality. Repressive measures were transformed into the art of governing. The people of Cameroon, seen as universally suspect, became the target of what was now a permanent war.

A much-weakened maquis

After five years of struggle against the French-Cameroonian forces, the UPC insurrection was in a perilous state in the early 1960s. This was notably the case on the internal front – that is, in the maquis that continued to fight in the western region in Mungo, Sanaga-Maritime and Wouri. Bombarded, tortured, hunted down, assailed by hunger and disease as much as by their adversaries, the rebel leaders struggled to coordinate their forces. Theoretically led by Martin Singap and still numbering several thousand fighters, the ALNK descended into chaos early in 1961. Communications between different maquis were becoming increasingly difficult and directives from the top often met with disarray on the ground. Singap's lieutenants were reluctant to abide by the general staff's decisions. Splits and internal quarrels were growing and autonomous armed bands, which, without any overall strategy, launched operations against the state forces, villagers or even other insurgent groups, even emerged. Sometimes short-circuited by his subordinates, Singap himself objected to instructions issued by the exiled UPC leadership.

The poisoning of Félix Moumié at the end of 1960 also did great damage to the external front – that is, to the UPC leaders scattered across the organisation's various offices around Africa: in Accra, Conakry, Rabat, Cairo and soon also Algiers. From these different centres they tried to take the UPC's message to the international scene and to gather support for the internal guerrilla movement at home. Recognised by progressive governments as the representative of the Cameroonian revolution, UPC president Moumié had managed to maintain a degree of unity at the head of the movement. His death changed all that. Strategic disagreements, clan struggles, generational conflicts, personal rivalries and, at times, ethnic rivalries all surged to the fore. Such was the suspicion among the exiles that the situation degenerated into open warfare from 1961 onwards, with some accusing others of trying to sabotage the revolutionary effort or even of secretly plotting with the imperialist enemy. Contemporary developments in the international situation, including the growing rivalry between Moscow and Beijing, served as a catalyst and fig-leaf justification for this internecine war. Dressing up their rivalries in pseudo-theoretical arguments and seeking the approval of more powerful sponsors, the 'pro-Chinese' UPC devoted inordinate energies to discrediting their 'pro-Soviet' UPC rivals, who responded in kind.

While the fighters on the internal front struggled in the mud in the face of constant fire from the French-Cameroonian army, the struggle of the UPC in exile – which claimed to represent the people of Kamerun – sank into an increasingly otherworldly abstraction. The only person who largely steered clear of these internal disagreements was Ernest Ouandié. The day after Moumié's death, the vice-president of the UPC decided to return clandestinely to Cameroon to relaunch the internal front. Arriving in the country a few weeks before Singap was killed by a Franco-Cameroonian patrol in September 1961, the man who would henceforth be known as 'Comrade Émile' was stunned to discover how far the maquis had broken up. With method and resolve, and relying on a few Cameroonian fighters who had been through political and military training abroad, he managed in just a few months to give the ALNK a coherent structure again and to reunite some of the dispersed maquis.

The reports from the police, army and intelligence services testify to the success of 'Comrade Émile' and his efforts. While in the preceding months these forces had grown in confidence, from 1962 they were rather more skittish. Informed of Ouandié's return, they had difficulty locating him and were even – wrongly – worried that foreigners might land in Cameroon in order to help the rebels. 'It's all starting!' fumed a French general who thought he had spotted FLN agents in the Cameroonian scrubland a few months after Algeria gained its independence. 'Soon there will be more of them all over French-speaking Africa.' Lauding the talents of the new leader of the internal rebellion as an 'organiser' and 'propagandist', Colonel Blanc, the man behind the scenes at the Ministry of the Cameroonian Armed Forces (FAC), also seemed especially on edge: 'The situation seems to me, if not alarming, at least serious,' he wrote in March 1963 in a secret report sent to the French government.

> Among the populations in the Mungo and Bamileke regions (a quarter of the [total] population) the rebels have more of an audience than the government does. The proof is in two facts: despite the blows dealt to it, the rebellion's recruitment has never been exhausted [and] never has the population spontaneously informed the forces of order.[1]

Until the early 1970s, the maquis survived in Mungo, in the West and, to a lesser degree, in Sanaga-Maritime. Ever on the move, Ouandié set up his command base in the Bamileke region, from where he and his men continued to stand firm against the regime for almost ten years. Despite some successes and, indeed, their unfailing determination, this decade of resistance seemed increasingly hopeless. Ouandié lost his last liaison officer, Emmanuel Fankam (alias 'Fermeté', 'steadfastness'), in 1964, a loss which cut him off almost completely from the rest of the world. Under constant attack from the French-Cameroonian troops, the ALNK's numbers dwindled inexorably.

The politics of fear and psychological warfare

In order to isolate Ouandié and his troops, the Cameroonian military and paramilitary forces – whose high-command structures long remained French – kept up their operations in what were called 'rebellion-infected zones'. 'Officially, the French forces are NON operational since 1 January 61,' observed a British secret report. In reality, 'they carry on operations under the cover name of training manoeuvres'.[2] It was in this context that from 1962 to 1964 Max Bardet, the helicopter pilot mentioned in the opening pages of this book, took part in the bloody but covert operations that he called 'controlled massacres'.

The central aim was, of course, to strike at the insurgents, to make their lives impossible, and to drive them from their hideouts. When captured, the rebels were systematically tortured and often executed, with their decapitated heads put on public view for days on end. This was an appalling practice, but one which became so common that the beheading of enemies was incorporated into the propaganda devised by the army itself. For example, this slogan was used during a psychological campaign in the Mungo region: 'Follow the example of this brave Cameroonian planter from Baré who saw the maquisards, immediately ran to tell the soldiers and a few minutes later all these gorillas [sic] were shot, decapitated and their heads displayed.'[3] To complete this mechanism, many public executions were organised in market squares or on communal sports fields. The villagers, including schoolchildren, were summoned to attend what the British embassy described in its confidential reports as 'grisly rituals'.[4] In Bafoussam, tens of thousands of people attended the execution on 3 January 1964 of Pierre Kamdem Niyim, the former Baham chief and former minister of health, who was accused of colluding with the maquis. This happened the same day as the executions of insurgent leaders Tankeu Noé in Douala and Makandepouthe in Edea.

In this way, the violence unleashed after the independence declaration was in fact deliberately kept alive in what were considered sensitive regions. For more than a decade, until the early 1970s, all manner of atrocities were the daily fare of Cameroonians in the West and Mungo regions. In accordance with the doctrine of countersubversive warfare, the target was not only the rebel movement itself but all those – men, women and children – suspected of doing the slightest thing to support it or provide it with supplies. Hence in 1965, the highest state authorities decided to 'subject to administrative internment, with a view to encouraging a switching of loyalties, parents who had one or more children in the maquis, or whose child(ren) were known to be rebels'.[5] The repression thus soon spread by the connections that could be established between one person and the next: one by one, all the inhabitants of the regions were subjected to the policy of terror that had been introduced in the late 1950s. Often, whole villages were targeted. There was a constant churn of massacres, perpetrated either by the supposed guardians of the law or by more or less autonomous village militias. There were many examples of this kind of collective punishment in Mungo, home to a large Bamileke community. In Nlohé at the end of 1961, in a district of Nkongsamba in 1963 and in Tombel in 1966, dozens, if not hundreds, of Bamileke inhabitants were murdered. The Tombel massacre in which, according to the authorities' confidential report, 236 people were killed and 1,000 wounded was clearly ethnic in character. As the on-the-ground investigation a few weeks later indicated: 'The massacre of Bamileke elements would appear to have taken place almost simultaneously in Nkeng, Suke, Ngap, Ngussi, Mahole, Peng, Ekonebe, Kupe and Mbonzie. It seemingly came a little late in Nyassosso. These are the names of neighbourhoods of Tombel and Bakossi villages five to nine kilometres apart . . . The Bakossi dwellings in the affected areas were spared and are emerging from the heaps of ashes.'⁶

If Cameroonian officials' confidential reports sometimes deplored what they described as 'massacres', 'carnage' or even acts of 'extermination', they tended to regard them as mere excesses. The authorities were in no hurry to intervene, even when they had been alerted to such abuses in advance, and showed little concern to punish those responsible, who thus enjoyed total impunity.

The ethnic hatreds vented by Cameroonian officials also bore some comparison to the rhetoric used by Jean Lamberton in March 1960 when he referred to the Bamileke people as a 'stone in the shoe'. The head of the SEDOC political police, Jean Fochivé, even called the Bamileke a 'plague'. Also telling is the attitude of Félix Sabal Lecco, who between 1964 and 1970 successively held the posts of prefect of Mungo and Wouri, federal inspector of the Coastal region, secretary of state for rural development and minister of justice. Still just before his death in 2010 he described his Bamileke compatriots in the following terms: 'There are so many of these people – they're like ants! – that they have to try and settle everywhere . . . What neighbourhood has no Bamileke? What town, what village, where is there no Bamileke in Cameroon? Not only in Cameroon, but all over the world! They are the Jews of Cameroon. You can't avoid the Bamileke phenomenon, it's not possible. You can't fight the Bamileke phenomenon.'[7]

To separate the 'healthy' population from 'contaminated' elements, and more generally to cordon off the Bamileke people, who had been labelled a fifth column, the villagisation policy pursued from 1960 became both widespread and institutionalised. According to the French ambassador Jean-Pierre Bénard, 'almost the entire population of the five *départements*' of the Bamileke region was resettled in this way. In May 1962, the ambassador noted that 'the face of the resettlements had changed. The temporary huts had often become semi-established . . . The schools and dispensaries that were operating eighteen months ago in dark, rickety shelters had been rebuilt: cement-coated walls and breeze-blocks, sheet metal roofs. The classrooms are large and bright. By concentrating the population, the resettlement has led to spectacular improvements in school attendance.'[8]

The real aim of concentration was to discipline the Bamileke population, which was seen, en bloc, as suspect. Here again, psychological warfare measures initially seen as temporary became established policy. As the rebellion waned in some areas, some of the civic guards were turned into 'heads of civic and psychological operations'. The idea was no longer simply to 'detoxify' the population and screen for suspicious behaviour. The aim now was re-education, in the strongest sense of the word: the region's inhabitants not only were pressured to repudiate their alleged 'subversive' tendencies but now had to pledge allegiance to the regime in Yaoundé – even publicly so. The training provided in the mid-1960s by the Cameroonian army's most senior officers, many of whom were French, testified to this growing obsession with 'psychological warfare'. During our research we found the text of lectures given to officers and non-commissioned officers operating in Mungo in 1967 as part of an 'information course on intelligence and psychological action'. The terms used in this 325-page document leave no doubt as to the lecturers' intentions. Almost every page contains references to 'crowd psychology', 'psychological penetration', 'changing public opinion', 'brainwashing' or even 'stuffing the skull'. Hailing the 'success' of these educational efforts, the minister of the Cameroon armed forces explained at the end of the course that he had decided to 'extend it to the other regions' of Cameroon.[9]

A people under a blanket of lead

In fact, by that point the psychological warfare *had* already been extended to the rest of Cameroon, in an entirely deliberate and coordinated fashion. For the regime's most senior officials, the treatment applied to the areas 'infested' with rebels was no longer to be seen as exceptional but as a model for Cameroon as a whole. The 1960s thus saw a contradictory development: the fight against subversion expanded as the rebellion weakened.

The nerve centre of this war on the people was the president's office, where Ahidjo took his decisions with a small clutch of aides – rarely neglecting to seek the French leadership's view, via Jacques Foccart. The Élysée was the real head of all the security structures which, created at the moment of independence, now formed the pillars of the regime. This obviously included the police force. Trained and supervised by France, it played a central role in controlling the population under the now-permanent state of emergency – requiring every citizen to obtain a pass every time they wished to cross the territory.

Then there were the armed forces, set up in 1959 and numbering almost fifteen thousand men over the decade that followed. Taking up almost 20 per cent of the national budget, making this the largest army in French-speaking Africa, its remit continually expanded: far from defending Cameroon against foreign aggression, it was mainly used to repress the 'enemy within', a term given the widest imaginable definition. Ultimately, it behaved like an army of occupation. It was also increasingly assigned to tasks not connected to security, especially tasks related to pursuing the regime's development policies (building roads, villages, hospitals and so on).

But Ahidjo's quest for 'order and security' most of all relied on the all-powerful intelligence service, the SEDOC, and the fearsome mixed mobile units (BMM), fanning out from their bases in Yaoundé, Douala, Edea, Nkongsamba, Bamenda, Kumba, Dschang and so on. Headed from 1962 by Fochivé, a police officer trained by the French intelligence services, the SEDOC – often described even by the most moderate historians as the Ahidjo regime's Gestapo – sowed terror across the country. Today, there are many accounts by the victims of this special police force, which dragged suspects from their beds in the middle of the night, on any number of pretexts, and took them *manu militari* to police stations, prisons or other makeshift torture chambers to inflict the most varied of abuses, sometimes for months on end. These methods included waterboarding, the 'swing', electrocution (the *gégène*), suffocation, mock executions, genital mutilation, depriving them of sleep or food and so on.

Practised by all parts of the armed forces, torture had become a means of governing the population. Fifty years on, many Cameroonians are still able to describe the abuses they suffered – or carried out – in remarkable detail. Those who escaped remember the cries and the pleading that could daily be heard from the barracks and police stations. 'You quickly get used to seeing the police and hearing prisoners being tortured,' said a Canadian who was working in Bafoussam at the time. 'It sounds crazy to say that.' The same man went on to explain that the gendarmes had their electrodes repaired at the local technical college. 'Everyone knew,' he concluded, pointing out that the school in question was part of the French mission.[10]

Those who did not die at the hands of their torturers were whisked off to the official prisons or, more often, to the appalling administrative detention and civic re-education centres built all over the country (the main ones being in Yoko, Tchollliré, Mantoum and Mokolo). These secret sites were designed in 1961 – in the words of the regime's éminence grise, Samuel Kamé – to 'take in individuals who had not been convicted by the courts but whose removal from healthy society could be justified by the imperatives of public order and security'.[11] Thousands of suspects were thus sent without trial to these centres where, deprived of everything and treated like animals, they underwent shock treatment, which lasted day and night sometimes for years on end, designed to bring them back onto the straight and narrow. One among the many examples of the contempt for the prisoners' lives was the so-called death-train scandal, which erupted when the Catholic Church condemned the death of twenty-five prisoners, who had suffocated in a freight train during their transfer from Douala to Yaoundé on 1 February 1962. The regime's only response was to suppress the newspaper *L'Effort catholique*, which had broken the story, and expel its editor, the French priest Pierre Fertin.

Showing that the regime did not target the armed rebels alone and that it fully intended to crush any potential troublemakers, the law was amended to criminalise all forms of dissent. This was the aim of the decree 'to repress subversion' of 12 March 1962. In practice, it banned the expression of any disagreement with the regime. 'The President has given a total character to the fight against the agents of subversion and against all those who might not fully espouse the regime's doctrine,' commented the French ambassador in a confidential report to the Foreign Ministry.[12] In fact, the first targets of this new legislation were the four main leaders of what remained of the legal opposition: as soon as the four men were convicted they were sent to an administrative internment centre in North Cameroon. Believing, however, that the 1962 decree was still too liberal, Ahidjo's office decided to tighten it further and extend it the following year, in particular by transferring cases of subversion from the criminal courts to the military tribunals. By now, the leaden blanket over Cameroon covered everything. Politics became a mere shadow play: the political opposition disappeared, journalism became a sham and a petrified Cameroonian people took refuge in silence.

The 'rational command of the masses'

Having fought the rebellion militarily, crushed the opposition, silenced journalists and, in short, made any form of protest illegal, the Cameroonian government gradually transformed the ruling party, which was also directly controlled by the president, into a single party. The Cameroonian National Union (UNC), which replaced the Cameroonian Union in 1966, completed the regime's repressive arsenal. The UNC was not a political party in the traditional sense. Explicitly inspired by fascist methods, it was structured on an ultra-hierarchical basis and integrated numerous paramilitary units. This machine of control made it possible to place each locality under intense surveillance, monitor the inhabitants, promote the deserving and punish the recalcitrant. From 1966 onwards, the UNC was the only authorised party, gradually creating a parallel state apparatus and allowing the regime's ideologues to tighten their grip on the administrative and security apparatus, which they still considered too lax. 'The structure of the national UNC party allows a rational command of the masses,' commented a delighted Captain Henri-Marcel Meno during the psychological-action course held in Nkongsamba in 1967. 'The party's various apparatuses offer unlimited possibilities in the field of organisation. In this way, we can dominate the population and, in due course, militarise it.'[13]

This was the regime's agenda: in order to 'purify the population', as one presidential order put it, it had to be 'mobilised', in the military sense. Monitored, controlled and regimented, the people of Cameroon were urged each day to prove their fealty to the regime, to renew their unwavering allegiance to the party and to sing the praises of the president himself. A cult of Ahidjo was skilfully orchestrated, with the head of state now cast as 'father of the nation'. Pressured to actively collaborate with the forces of order and to spread the single party's slogans, they were summoned to denounce anyone who showed the slightest doubt. Since silence was itself considered suspicious, reporting on others gradually became the ultimate mark of patriotism, and also served to bulk out the files of the SEDOC (renamed the Directorate of Studies and Documentation, DIRDOC, in 1969).

Economic policy also responded to this need for general mobilisation: official propaganda proclaimed the need to win the 'battle for development'. Here again, the Cameroonian people, judged to be too 'backward', 'lazy' and lacking in 'zeal for work', were viewed with suspicion by the barons of the regime. The latter were quick to seize upon psychological weapons, to which they were now unquestioningly committed, to stir up the people's energies. In 1967, Ahidjo's speech at the inauguration of a 'pioneer village', built with army support on the model of the Israeli kibbutz, illustrated the regime's philosophy well:

Committed youth, enrolled youth, youth steeped in the ideology of the party which places development and national construction at the heart of its programme, it is they who must be the apostle of this psychological change of going back to the land, of the love of work; it is they who must stimulate it, promote it, propagate it.[14]

The same message was applied to all categories of citizens (women, the elderly, schoolchildren, soldiers, planters, shopkeepers and so on).

These people, it should be pointed out, voted en masse for the single party's candidate at every systematically rigged election. In the presidential election of March 1965, Ahidjo was re-elected with 100 per cent of the votes cast. He managed to repeat this score in 1970, 1975 and 1980, with an over-99-per-cent turnout in each instance.

So, while the rebellion disappeared almost completely from official discourse, the techniques that had been introduced in the late 1950s to eradicate it were continually extended to the rest of the population. By the end of the following decade, the war had become permanent, generalised and institutionalised. When, in 1966, some UPC exiles took advantage of the establishment of a Marxist regime in Congo-Brazzaville to attempt a military incursion into southern Cameroon, they were silently crushed by the Cameroonian army. This silence was broken temporarily when Ernest Ouandié was arrested in August 1970. But it was only because a Catholic bishop, Albert Ndongmo (1926–92), was accused of helping him that the affair came to international public attention (see box). The few foreign observers who still followed events in Cameroon discovered, with some surprise, that the armed resistance had been ongoing for more than a decade.

1970–71: the Ndongmo–Ouandié affair

On 18 August 1970, Ernest Ouandié, leader of the nationalist maquis since 1961 and the last major pro-independence leader still in hiding, was arrested. This event, which marked the end of any prospect of insurrection in Cameroon, owed to the combination of two strategies: that of Ouandié and his supporters looking for a way out of the maquis; and that of the regime which was trying to track him down. Albert Ndongmo, the enigmatic bishop of Nkongsamba (Mungo), played a central role in this race.

Since 1965, Ahidjo's regime had secretly sent Ndongmo to negotiate Ouandié's defection. But this failed, as the meeting between the two men in 1966 instead resulted in this dissident bishop rallying behind the maquis leader. On the radar of the authorities, who suspected him of plotting a coup d'état, Ndongmo was approached by a group of internationalist anti-colonialists, the Solidarité network, led by the Egyptian Communist Henri Curiel (1914–78). Solidarité's ambition was to exfiltrate Ouandié, whose position in the maquis was an isolated dead-end, in order to continue the struggle peacefully in exile. To achieve this, the network put Bishop Ndongmo in touch with the UPC in exile in Algiers. Solidarité even sent men to the English-speaking region of Cameroon to organise the operation to get Ouandié through Nigeria to Switzerland. But Ndongmo, who was being closely watched by the security forces, unwittingly led the military onto Ouandié's trail. Urgently summoned by the Vatican, Ndongmo disappeared just as he was meant to hand Ouandié over to the Solidarité men. Abandoned by the bishop, the insurgent leader was forced to surrender to the Cameroonian authorities. Despite threats against him, Ndongmo returned to Cameroon after his meeting at the Vatican and was arrested as soon as he got off the plane.

Since both men were originally from the West, the Ndongmo–Ouandié affair turned into a hunt for a 'Bamileke plot'. In the course of the investigation, dozens of personalities from all walks of life, including senior members of the regime, were suspected of having participated in an imaginary coup d'état, arrested and tortured. After forced 'confessions' were broadcast on the radio, Ouandié, Ndongmo and a few others were tried and sentenced to death. Despite an international campaign launched by Solidarité activists, Ouandié was shot in Bafoussam town square on 15 January 1971, along with two of his comrades. As for Bishop Ndongmo, his sentence was commuted to life imprisonment, and he, like other suspects – whether convicted or not – spent long years in sinister administrative internment camps.

This judicial farce briefly turned the spotlight back onto Cameroon's dictatorship.[15] In 1972, it prompted the famous Cameroonian writer Mongo Beti, who lived in France, to publish a book in which he denounced the Ahidjo regime and what he called the 'Foccartist mafia'. *Main basse sur le Cameroun*, published by François Maspero, was immediately banned and its copies seized. It was not authorised for publication in France until 1977.

But everything soon returned to normal. Just three weeks after Ouandié's public execution in Bafoussam town square on 15 January 1971, and while Bishop Ndongmo was being sent to the Tcholliré re-education centre in North Cameroon, French president Georges Pompidou, who was on a tour of Africa, made an official visit to Yaoundé. When a Cameroonian journalist asked him during his press conference why France had not itself adopted a one-party system, Pompidou indulged in a little humour. 'I may not have the authority of President Ahidjo, so my success may not be total,' he quipped, under the watchful eye of Foccart. The French president added with a rhetorical flourish: 'To be serious, I don't think we can expect a government – a democratic government as I understand it, one that respects individual rights – in the same way everywhere.'[16]

The triumph of the 'Françafrique' system in Cameroon

With these words, the French president showed how laid-back he was about Cameroon's regime, even though it had just assassinated the last great resistance leader after a parody of a trial. Pompidou was free to express this feeling because in this moment nothing seemed able to threaten the neocolonial pact that the French and Cameroonian leaders had sealed ten years previously. The 'Françafrique' system put in place at the end of the 1950s was also made permanent, in Cameroon as in the rest of France's backyard.

Under the guise of 'French–African friendship' – and thanks to the many agreements that Paris had Yaoundé sign at the moment of independence (on defence, cooperation, monetary and economic matters, the maintenance of the CFA franc and the French currency zone and so on) – this neocolonial system enabled France to maintain its tutelage over Cameroon. It did this by subcontracting the management of day-to-day affairs to the small elite that it had placed at the head of the country, who in turn took full advantage of the privileges that this situation guaranteed to them. By protecting Cameroon's leaders against the risks of instability and thereby ensuring the local elite a continued rent on their subordination, official France could thus unashamedly defend its interests while presenting Cameroon as fully sovereign.

But the French had not disappeared from the Cameroonian landscape – far from it. The repressive apparatus was still largely controlled by them. In 1971, *most* senior officers in the Cameroonian army were of French nationality, and all the others had been trained in the former colonial power's military institutions.[17] The civil service was in a similar situation: while in 1960 there were 1,800 colonial civil servants, 1,314 French *coopérants* were working directly or indirectly in the Cameroonian administration in 1976.[18] Occupying key positions in all of the country's institutions (the tax administration, education, police, the justice system and so on), these French officials appeared to many observers as a real fifth column at the heart of the Cameroonian state machine. This was particularly the case in economic matters, as historian Richard Joseph noted in 1978:

> for several years after independence, French experts not only drew up the 'development plans', but were able to ensure that the country

continued in the right direction by their predominance as 'advisers' in all the government's economic ministries as well as within Ahidjo's ruling circle.[19]

We can thus easily imagine how well served French economic interests were in this country, which in the early 1970s was considered the third richest in French-speaking Africa (after Côte d'Ivoire and Senegal). In fact, the main beneficiaries of development aid would almost always be French companies. In the name of encouraging foreign investment, French business chiefs benefited from countless tax breaks and favourable customs arrangements, thus preventing the development of Cameroonian industry itself. Fifteen years after Cameroon's political independence, 97 per cent of industrial concerns on its soil were European-owned, with French bosses easily in the lead (as in the mining sector, where 90 per cent of the capital was held by French interests). This produced yawning inequalities: while Cameroonians made up 93.7 per cent of the non-agricultural workforce, the French occupied 82 per cent of the much-better-paid senior management roles. At the beginning of the 1980s, the nine thousand or so French nationals then present in Cameroon, as the magazine *African Affairs* put it, 'continue to dominate virtually all sectors of the commanding heights of the economy, much as they did before independence. French settlers control 55 per cent of the modern sector of the Cameroonian economy, and their control of the country's banking system is complete and total.'[20]

Cameroon thus offered a template of what a neocolonial economy could be: the former colonial power massively repatriating its capital, in the form of profits or salaries, while leaving only the crumbs to the local populations. The situation got even worse with the extraction of Cameroonian oil, discovered in the mid-1950s under the country's territorial waters. Although extraction was deemed unprofitable at the time, the boom in oil prices following the 1973 oil crisis allowed operations to get going in 1977. But this did not benefit the Cameroonian population in any way. Cameroon's oil revenues were handled 'off-budget' and placed in obscure foreign bank accounts (in France, Switzerland and the United States); they swelled the profits of the French company Elf and the personal coffers of a handful of French-Cameroonian executives. According to a 2009 study, no less than $10.7 billion in oil revenues thus 'evaporated' between 1977 and 2006. The authors note, 'This amount may have been privately appropriated although it is not clear which part was appropriated by oil companies and government officials.'[21]

Historians will have to determine the exact role played by the Élysée Palace and Elf, an armed wing of Françafrique, in Ahidjo's sudden resignation in 1982. Although there were no forewarnings of his departure – he had been 'triumphantly re-elected' only two years earlier – the dictator, who was said to be ill, suddenly handed over his place to the man who had been his prime minister since 1975: Paul Biya, a regime apparatchik born in 1933.

For many observers, this hasty succession had less to do with the Yaoundé strongman's health condition than with the left's rise to power in France for the first time in the history of the Fifth Republic, founded in 1958. Did François Mitterrand, who had reached the presidency a few months earlier, seek to oust Ahidjo, who was too close to the French right, in order to install his own networks in Yaoundé? Others see it as a manoeuvre directed by the chiefs of the French state oil company Elf – though the two theories are also compatible. On this reading, enticed by the oil deposits discovered off the coast of English-speaking Cameroon, the oil giant ousted Ahidjo in order to place a more pliant figure at the head of the country. In the mid-1990s, Loïk Le Floch-Prigent, who was CEO of this French multinational from 1989 to 1993, gave credence to this theory when, during the politico-financial Elf scandal, he revealed the role that he had played at the time: 'It was thanks to Elf that France maintained a presence in

French-speaking Africa and extended it to other countries.' Citing the cases of Gabon and Congo, Le Floch-Prigent also mentioned Cameroon, 'where President Biya only came to power with Elf's support, to keep a lid on the country's English-speaking community'.[22]

In any case, Paul Biya became master of Cameroon in 1982. This same man still reigns forty-three years later, without a plan or vision, over a country plagued by corruption, disorganisation and inequality. Admittedly, the regime seems to have become somewhat more flexible: some of the counter-subversive legislation adopted in the 1960s has been ditched; the one-party system has been abolished; and the press enjoys some limited freedom. But this is no more than a façade, as real power remains in the hands of a small caste of wealthy individuals affiliated with the presidential party, the Cameroonian People's Democratic Movement (RDPC), the direct heir to Ahidjo's UNC. The slightest serious protest is bloodily suppressed, as in February 2008 when the security forces – still obsessed with 'subversion' – crushed a vast social protest movement against the high cost of living and the Biya regime's unending rule. The protests were broken up at the cost of around a hundred deaths and thousands of arrests.

Most Western governments openly criticise the regime's authoritarian methods, as well as the sham elections it periodically organises. From de Gaulle and Pompidou in the 1960s and 1970s through Giscard, Mitterrand and Chirac to Sarkozy and Hollande in the 2010s and Macron in the 2020s, France has been a staunch supporter of this regime. France is as committed to the regime's continuation as it is unconcerned about the human rights abuses the regime routinely commits. Every now and then, the French authorities pout their lips in disapproval and say that they prefer 'friendly pressure' to 'thundering condemnations'. But in practice, nothing has changed: Biya is still welcomed with open arms at the Élysée Palace and French leaders line up to shake hands in Yaoundé. Displayed like trophies on the official website of the Cameroonian presidency, the photos showing their delighted faces under the panelling of the Etoudi Palace, where they are welcomed by the Cameroonian autocrat, say more than their non-committal declarations of intent ever could.

Under the pretext of 'the war on terror', the pact between Paris and Yaoundé even seems to have been strengthened in recent years, after the north of Cameroon came under attack from Boko Haram. This was a godsend for Biya, who in 2014 had no hesitation in drawing unseemly parallels between the anticolonial movement of the 1950s and 1960s, which fought for the liberation of Cameroon, and the jihadist sect of the 2010s, which instead dreams of subjecting Cameroon to a theocratic dictatorship.

The repression of the secessionist movement in the English-speaking provinces of Cameroon has further tested the strength of Franco-Cameroonian relations since 2017. While the Yaoundé regime refuses any form of dialogue with the separatists, its French partners, content with formal remonstrances, have not suspended their police and military cooperation with the Republic of Cameroon. It is an attitude not without consequences for the evolution of a conflict that has caused the death of 6,000 people and the forced displacement of 700,000, according to a report published by Amnesty International in July 2023.[23]

Describing any form of dissent, whatever its nature, as 'terrorist', and thus securing the military, diplomatic and financial support of the French authorities, determined to prevent any 'destabilisation' in Cameroon, Paul Biya should be able to live peacefully in power until the end of his days. Paris is watching over him.

Epilogue: A Stubborn Past, an Impatient Future

During a state visit to Yaoundé in 2015, François Hollande spoke of the 'extremely tormented episodes' that had surrounded Cameroon's independence. Why would he say such a thing? While these words went almost unnoticed in France, they were greeted with a certain relief by the Cameroonian public. For the first time, the highest authorities of the French state, in the person of the president of the Republic, recognised that something had indeed happened in Cameroon at the time of decolonisation. Referring to repression in Sanaga-Maritime and the Bamileke region, Hollande even said he was ready to 'open the history books [and] the archives'.

Seven years later, on 16 July 2022, François Hollande's successor, Emmanuel Macron, also visiting Yaoundé, likewise announced the beginning of a 'fact-finding process' and promised to open the archives to a memorial commission, made up of French and Cameroonian researchers and artists. 'Historians have looked into this past: they tell us that a conflict took place, the word *war* was used,' he said. 'It's up to historians to shed light on the past.' This strategy has enabled him to postpone any recognition of France's crimes by at least two years, the time allotted for the commission to deliver its report. It also conceals the fact that historians have exploited widely accessible archives for decades, clearly establishing most of the basic facts.

The commission, led by the French historian Karine Ramondy, which presented its report to presidents Macron and Biya at the end of January 2025, unsurprisingly confirmed the conclusions of earlier historians: France did wage a 'war' in Cameroon during the 1950s and '60s, causing tens of thousands of deaths and using the same tactics it had used in Algeria: torture, bombing, villagisation, political assassinations, psychological warfare, and so on. The report, written by fourteen French and Cameroonian historians, drawing on previously known archives and newly declassified documents, was met with scepticism in Cameroon. Beyond offering a few new insights, despite its thousand pages, the report was paired with an 'artistic initiative' led by the Cameroonian singer Blick Bassy, tasked with popularising the commission's findings and fostering Franco-Cameroonian 'memory reconciliation' through a wide range of cultural devices: films, songs, murals, video games, cooking workshops, hairdressing contests, 3-D virtual immersions into reconstituted maquis, and more.[1]

Hence the question: does this commission reflect a real desire to 'shed light' on the Cameroon War and to initiate a genuine policy of recognition and reparations, or is it simply another PR gambit on the part of a French president eager to turn historical disputes – with Rwanda, Algeria and now Cameroon – into illustrations of his 'disruptive method'?

In any case, it is clear that the 'remembrance initiatives' undertaken by French leaders in recent years are part of a new soft-power strategy. At a time when 'anti-French sentiment' is spreading across Africa and rival powers encroach on France's neocolonial backyard, Paris is on the lookout for new ways to demonstrate its goodwill. The resulting commissions, whose members are directly appointed by the Élysée, give the illusion that a page of history has been turned. And timid recognition of a few past crimes, doled out in dribs and drabs, gives the impression that there is nothing left to be explored. As the historian Noureddine Amara points out, the 'reconciliation' called for by Emmanuel Macron looks more like an exercise in 'memorial pacification', aimed at silencing those who reject the anaesthetising interpretations promoted by official history.[2]

To understand the Élysée's embarrassment or caution, it is important to bear in mind that the war in Cameroon does not belong to a bygone era that can be filed away in history books like old papers in a drawer, the better to forget them. Rather, this war remains a burning issue for today. How can we understand postcolonial Cameroon if we overlook the fact that it was born through war? How can we conceive Cameroon's future if we do not understand that this war, which officially never existed and therefore has not yet ended, continues in the form of a despotic regime that still rules the country even today? How can we believe in the Franco-Cameroonian friendship that public officials have boasted about for decades when we know that these words conceal a system that has perpetuated a steeply unequal relationship?

Faced with increasingly pressing demands over the historical memory of this conflict, French authorities are caught in a tangle of contradictions. The first, perhaps the most important, is the divide between myth and historical reality. Although France likes to describe itself as the 'homeland of human rights', it stubbornly refuses to take an honest look at chapters of the past that contradict this flattering self-image. The 2005 call made by a handful of MPs for history textbooks to reflect the 'positive aspects' of colonisation and the obsessive rejection of any form of 'contrition' are just two examples of France's difficulty breaking out of self-mythology and essentialist narratives. No, France is not *naturally* generous-spirited: like all imperialist nations, when its material interests are at stake, it has never hesitated to trample on the grand principles it claims to represent.

The decolonisation of the former 'French Black Africa' is also part of this national mythology, since it is generally described as a peaceful process through which France shepherded its colonies to independence in a completely disinterested manner. But this story is undermined by all those who try to shed light on the bloody events that punctuated the period in question, from the Thiaroye massacre in 1944 to the repression of the Malagasy uprising in 1947 to the punishment of Ivorian political activists in 1948–50 and Operation Écouvillon in Mauritania ten years later. These too-often-overlooked episodes – and so many others – belie official accounts and prove that from Paris's perspective the decolonisation of French Africa did not spell an end to French influence over the region. The neocolonial dispensation known as 'Françafrique' would make sure of that.

Here we see the other contradiction that French leaders in recent decades have walked into. While they constantly swear that they have broken with Françafrique, in practice their policies have consisted, at best, in reforming the traditional instruments of France's African policy to adapt them to the spirit of the times.[3] In a way, since the turn of the twenty-first century France has found itself in a situation comparable to that of the 1940s and '50s, when its leaders decided to reform the colonial system in order not to 'lose everything'. Today, it is that system's successor – notwithstanding periodic reports of its demise – that refuses to give up the ghost. Shaken by globalisation, migration, ever greater access to information and the emergence of new players on the international scene, African societies – particularly the youth – are losing interest in the former colonial powers. They are looking elsewhere, to the United States, Canada, Russia, China or Brazil, and inventing new ways of living, fighting and resisting.

France, which still entertains fantasies of grandeur and has every intention of 'retaining its presence in Africa', has thus fallen into its own trap. It is caught between two eras. One is a stubborn past, that of a Françafrique forged during the Cold War and decolonisation. The other is a future that is growing impatient, driven by younger generations fed up with the old autocrats who serve as functionaries for the former colonial powers. The way in which the people of

Tunisia (in 2011) and Burkina Faso (in 2014) swept aside their respective dictators, Zine el-Abidine Ben Ali and Blaise Compaoré – both great friends of France – speaks to this changing of the times. So too the military coups which have shaken the Sahel since 2021, bringing to power juntas hostile to Paris in Mali, Burkina Faso and Niger.

Like other countries, Cameroon illustrates in its own way the widening gap between Africa's elites and the continent's peoples. Cameroonians are ruled by a president who is ninety-two years of age at the time of this English edition and who spends astronomical sums on palatial stays in Europe. But the ordinary population, half of whom are aged under eighteen, live in extremely difficult conditions, with an average income of less than €100 a month according to the World Bank. France's leaders are well aware that Biya, the direct heir to Ahidjo, under whom he served as prime minister from 1975 to 1982, cannot last forever. They must now choose: continue to support the authoritarian regime in Yaoundé, whose only legitimacy rests on rigged elections, a sprawling system of corruption and the routine repression of political opponents, or finally listen to a people who wish, like all others, to have a say in determining their own fate.

Today, Biya's system is running out of steam and impatience is growing in every corner of the country. Cameroon, whose English-speaking regions have been the scene of bloody armed conflict for almost ten years, is on the verge of a fresh explosion. French authorities, having taken a lesson from events in Tunisia, Burkina Faso, Mali, Niger, Gabon and most recently Senegal, are all the more conscious of this as they see an anti-French movement rising across the continent. They know that, having kept silent for so long about their own actions and those of the Françafrique-style regimes they have lifted to power in recent decades, there is a real risk that they will be among the prime targets of a popular revolt in Cameroon. The war that has been buried for too long could then suddenly resurface. Sooner or later, all crimes must be paid for.

Archives and Their Abbreviations

ADD: Archives départementales de Dschang
ANB: Archives nationales de Buea
ANOM: Archives nationales d'outre-mer (Aix-en-Provence)
ANY: Archives nationales de Yaoundé
APO: Archives provinciales de l'Ouest (Bafoussam)
Bibliothèque du DEFAP – Service protestant de mission (Paris)
CADN: Centre des archives diplomatiques (Nantes)
CARAN: Centre d'accueil et de recherche des Archives nationales
(Paris)
CHETOM: Centre historique des territoires d'outre-mer (Fréjus)
Fonds Maurice Couve de Murville au Centre historique de Sciences
Po (Paris)
PCF: Parti communiste français (Bobigny)
SHD: Service historique de la défense (Vincennes)
TNA: The British National Archives (Kew)

Notes

Introduction

1. Thomas Deltombe, Manuel Domergue and Jacob Tatsitsa, *Kamerun! Une guerre cachée aux origines de la Françafrique, 1948–1971*, Paris 2011.
2. Max Bardet and Nina Thellier, *OK cargo! La saga africaine d'un pilote d'hélicoptère*, Paris 1988.
3. Constantin Melnik, *La Mort était leur mission*, Paris 1995, p. 195.
4. 'Rapport du général Dio pour le haut commissaire au Cameroun', 'Enseignements tirés des opérations de rétablissement de l'ordre en Sanaga-Maritime', 30 April 1957, SHD 6H/62.
5. Major F. Aerts, 'Le renseignement en AEF', 9 July 1958, p. 20, SHD 6H/30.
6. Letter from Max Briand to the chief of the defence staff, 5 January 1960, SHD 6H/239.
7. Frantz Fanon, 'Toward the Liberation of Algeria', in *Toward the African Revolution: Political Essays*, New York 1967, pp. 81, 97.
8. Charles Lacheroy, 'Guerre révolutionnaire et arme psychologique', talk delivered on 2 July 1957; reproduced in Charles Lacheroy, *Discours et conférences*, ed. Anne-Catherine Schmidt-Trimborn, Metz 2012, pp. 171–200.
9. General Max Briand, 'Rapport sur les opérations militaires au Cameroun en 1960', 7 April 1961, SHD 6H/240.
10. M. A. Goodfellow, British Embassy, Yaoundé, to J. Mellon, West and Central Africa Dept, 'Report and figures of civilian casualties in Cameroon between Jan. 1962 and June 1962', 22 July 1964, Foreign Office, 371/176876.
11. André Blanchet, 'Le Cameroun 1962: Pacification et réunification', talk delivered to the Groupe d'études des problèmes africains, Centre d'étude de politique étrangère, 26 October 1962, pp. 7–8, private archives of André Blanchet, Académie des sciences d'outre-mer.

12. Cited in Meredith Terretta, *Nation of Outlaws, State of Violence: Nationalism, Grassfields Tradition, and State Building in Cameroon*, Athens 2014, p. 250.

13. Charles Lacheroy, 'Leçon de l'action viêt-minh et communisme en Indochine, ou une leçon de guerre révolutionnaire' (1954); reproduced in Lacheroy, *Discours et conférences*, pp. 111–46.

14. Ruben Um Nyobè, 'Rapport présenté au IIᵉ Congrès statutaire de l'UPC', Eséka, 29 September 1952; cited in Achille Mbembe, *Écrits sous maquis*, Paris 1989, pp. 81–2.

15. Cited in Alain d'Aix and Jean-Claude Burger, 'Contre-censure: Main basse sur le Cameroun' (documentary), Inform'Action Films, Quebec 1976 (see informactionfilms.com).

16. Mongo Beti, *Main basse sur le Cameroun*, Paris 1977 [1972], p. 6.

17. A surprise guest played a crucial role in this initiative: the academic Achille Mbembe, who wrote the preface to the French edition of this book. Highly critical of the French authorities at the time, the Cameroonian historian became one of President Macron's advisers from 2021 and wrote, at the request of the 'Elysée, a report aimed at laying the foundations for a 'new relationship' between France and Africa. Following this widely publicised report, Macron took the initiative of announcing, in 2022, the establishment of a Franco-Cameroonian 'memorial commission', led by the French historian Karine Ramondy and the Cameroonian singer Blick Bassy. For a critical look at this initiative, see Thomas Deltombe, Manuel Domergue and Jacob Tatsitsa, 'Guerre du Cameroun: Une commission d'historiens, pour quoi faire?', *Afrique XXI*, 16 September 2022.

1. Preludes

1. 'La souveraineté', *Togo-Cameroun*, March–April 1931, p. 180.

2. Cited in 'Memoirs of William Alleyne Robinson, 1960–1961', Bodleian Library of Commonwealth and African Studies at Rhodes House, Oxford, GB 162 MSS. Afr.s.2033.

3. Blaise Alfred Ngando, *La France au Cameroun, 1916–1939: Colonialisme ou mission civilisatrice?*, Paris 2002, pp. 111–14.

4. Achille Mbembe, *La Naissance du maquis dans le Sud-Cameroun, 1920–1960: Histoire des usages de la raison en colonie*, Paris 1996, p. 35.

5. Philippe Nken Ndjeng, *L'Idée nationale dans le Cameroun francophone, 1920–1960*, Paris 2012.

6. Emmanuel Tchumtchoua, *De la Jeucafra à l'UPC: L'éclosion du nationalisme camerounais*, Yaoundé 2006; Janvier Onana, 'Entrées en politique: Voies

promotionnelles de l'apprentissage et de l'insertion politiques "indigènes" dans l'État colonial au Cameroun. L'expérience de la Jeucafra', *Polis*, vol. 7, 1999–2000.

7. Guy Georgy, *Le Petit Soldat de l'empire*, Paris 1992, p. 33.
8. Eugène-Jean Duval, *Le Sillage militaire de la France au Cameroun, 1914–1964*, Paris 2004, p. 157.
9. 'PV de renseignement', 14 December 1945, ANY APA/13306.
10. Cited in Léon Kaptué, 'Grèves, émeutes et répression au Cameroun: Les événements de septembre 1945 à Douala', *Terroirs*, no. 2, January 1995, p. 97.

2. The Confrontation Takes Shape (1948–54)

1. Pierre Divol, 'Synthèse de l'implantation de l'UPC', 26 March 1955, ANY 2AC/8341.
2. Ruben Um Nyobè, 'Rapport présenté au IIe Congrès statutaire de l'UPC', Eséka, 29 September 1952; cited in Achille Mbembe, *Écrits sous maquis*, Paris 1989, pp. 81–2.
3. Report presented to the UPC steering committee, 9 December 1951, cited in Ruben Um Nyobè, *Le Problème national kamerunais*, Paris 1984, p. 128.
4. Frederick Cooper, *Africa since 1940*, Cambridge 2002, p. 49.
5. Guy Georgy, *Le Petit Soldat de l'empire*, Paris 1992.
6. Cited in Bernard de Gélis, *Lignes de partage*, Paris 2001, p. 184.
7. Pierre Divol, 'Synthèse de l'implantation de l'UPC'.
8. Cited in Bakang Ba Tonje, *L'Indépendance réelle d'abord. Stratégies et actions de l'UPC du 10 avril 1948 au 12 février 1991*, Douala 2007, p. 69.
9. AFP, 31 October 1952; cited in Ruben Um Nyobè, 'Les conditions historiques du mouvement de libération nationale', *Cahiers internationaux*, no. 53, February 1954.
10. 'Liste des notabilités africaines du Sud-Cameroun', SHD 15H/52.
11. Cited in Achille Mbembe, *La Naissance du maquis dans le Sud-Cameroun, 1920–1960: Histoire des usages de la raison en colonie*, Paris 1996, p. 254.
12. Bloc démocratique camerounais, 'L'heure du choix a sonné!', 30 April 1955, p. 14, PCF Archives.
13. *Jeune Afrique*, no. 1510, 11 December 1989; cited in Emmanuel Tchumtchoua, *De la Jeucafra à l'UPC: L'éclosion du nationalisme camerounais*, Yaoundé 2006, p. 186.
14. Direction des affaires économiques et du plan, 'Note sur la souveraineté française', 11 December 1950, ANY 1AC/168/1.
15. See Thomas Deltombe, *L'Afrique d'abord! Quand François Mitterrand voulait sauver l'Empire français*, Paris 2024.

16. 'Synthèse historique: L'évolution politique et des partis politiques dans la zone de défense AOF-Togo. Notice à l'usage des officiers du 2e bureau', 2nd trimester 1954, p. 89, SHD 6H/238.

17. 'Rapport moral et d'orientation présenté par Houphouët-Boigny, président du mouvement', Comité de coordination du RDA, 8 July 1955, p. 6, ANOM, 1 Aff-Pol 2246/B3.

18. François Mitterrand, *Présence française et abandon*, Paris 1957, p. 179 *sq.*

19. Pierre Divol, 'Synthèse de l'implantation de l'UPC'.

20. Captain Balladur, 'Incidents au Cameroun, mai 1955', SHD 6H/237.

21. ANY 1AC/91/8; cited in Daniel Abwa, *Commissaires et hauts commissaires de la France au Cameroun (1916–1960)*, Yaoundé 2000, p. 364.

3. 'A Smaller Version of Algeria' (1955–58)

1. Niccolò Machiavelli, *The Prince*, translated by Tim Parks, London 2009, p. 69.

2. Roland Pré, 'Politique générale de lutte contre les organisations politiques du Cameroun noyautés par le Parti communiste (UPC, JDC, USCC, UDEFEC)', memo no. 273, 4 February 1955, ANY 1AC/1969.

3. Charles Lacheroy, 'Leçon de l'action viêt-minh et communisme en Indochine, ou une leçon de guerre révolutionnaire' (1954); reproduced in Charles Lacheroy, *Discours et conférences*, ed. Anne-Catherine Schmidt-Trimborn, Metz 2012, pp. 111–46.

4. Roland Pré, 'Télégramme du haut commissaire au ministère de la France d'outre-mer', Douala, 30 May 1955, CAOM Aff-Pol 3337.

5. Grégoire Momo, 'Informations sur le terrorisme en pays Bamiléké', unpublished MS, 1986, Grégoire Momo's private archives, Dschang.

6. 'La répression aurait coûté: Cent tués, plusieurs centaines de blessés, trois cents arrestations, des déportations', *L'Humanité*, 8 June 1955.

7. Cited in Richard A. Joseph, *Radical Nationalism in Cameroun: Social Origins of the UPC Rebellion*, Oxford 1977, p. 246.

8. Roland Pré, 'La situation au Cameroun. Recherche et définition d'une politique', 6 April 1956, SHD 10T/180.

9. Georgette Elgey, *La République des tourmentes*, vol. 1, Paris 1992, p. 532.

10. Cited in Simon Nken, *La gestion de l'UPC. De la solidarité idéologique à la division stratégique de cadres du mouvement nationaliste camerounais, 1948–1962*, PhD thesis, Univerity of Paris, 2006, p. 78.

11. Letter from Félix Moumié to Pierre Braun, 2 February 1956, PCF Archives.

12. Authors' interview with Philippe Antoine, Paris, 30 December 2009.

13. Captain Gabriel Haulin, 'Compte rendu d'une opération ayant été effectuée le 31.12.1956 près d'Edéa', SHD 6H/239.

14. Ruben Um Nyobè, 'Comment le massacre des Kamerunais a été préparé et consommé par le gouvernement français', 3 January 1957; cited in Achille Mbembe, *Écrits sous maquis*, Paris 1989, p. 186.

15. General Dio, 'Enseignements tirés des opérations de rétablissement de l'ordre en Sanaga-Maritime', 30 April 1957, SHD 6H/62.

16. Daniel Doustin, 'Note sur les événements actuels au Cameroun', n.d., CADN FHCC/6.

17. Ibid.

18. Paul Villatoux and Marie-Catherine Villatoux, *La République et son armée face au 'péril subversif': Guerre et action psychologiques, 1945–1960*, Paris 2005, pp. 273–4; Caroline Elkins, *Imperial Reckoning: The Untold Story of Britain's Gulag in Kenya*, New York 2005.

19. Cited in Gaëlle Leroy and Valérie Osouf, 'Cameroun: Autopsie d'une indépendance, (documentary), Program 33, 2007.

20. 'Rapport de sûreté du 1er au 28 février 1961', p. 15, Dschang Departmental Archives.

21. Authors' interview with Roland Barachette, Paris, 13 October 2009.

22. 'PV de la réunion du 23 mars 1958 dans le bureau du lieutenant-colonel Lamberton', p. 12, SHD 6H/246.

23. Jean Lamberton, 'La pacification de la Sanaga-Maritime: Cameroun décembre 1957–janvier 1959', Centre militaire d'information et de spécialisation pour l'outre-mer (CMISOM), 18 February 1960.

24. Authors' interview with Roland Barachette, Paris, 13 October 2009.

25. 'JMO du groupe de gendarmerie du Cameroun', 1st semester 1958, SHD 6H/109.

26. Frank Garbely, 'L'assassinat de Félix Roland Moumié: L'Afrique sous contrôle' (documentary), Triluna/TSR/Arte, 2005.

27. Letter from Ralph Gray to Commissioner J. O. Field (Buea), 12 July 1958, TNA CO 554 1764.

28. Report of a meeting with the consul Maxime Huré in Lagos, 12 July 1958, TNA CO 554 1764.

4. Stolen Independence (1959–60)

1. Cited in Jacques Marseille, *Empire colonial et capitalisme français: Histoire d'un divorce*, Paris 2005, p. 492.

2. Letter from Daniel Doustin to Xavier Torré, 23 April 1958, CADN FAFC/43.

3. Letter from Daniel Doustin to Jean Chapperon, 28 February 1958, CADN FAFC/43.
4. General René Cogny, 'Mesures à prendre en cas d'aggravation', 21 September 1959, SHD 6H/266.
5. Cited in 'Rapport de sûreté du 11 au 15 juillet 1958', pp. 27–8, APO 1AC/158.
6. 'Nouveau projet de convention franco-camerounaise relative à la défense, à l'ordre public et à l'emploi de la gendarmerie'; cited in letter from General Le Puloch to General Garbay, 'Accords franco-camerounais', 13 September 1958, SHD 6H/63.
7. Letter from Daniel Doustin to Jean Chapperon, 28 February 1958.
8. Interview with Pierre Stibbe, 'Le Cameroun à la veille de l'indépendance', France observateur, 26 March 1959.
9. Files 'BAG200043: Cameroun 1958–1960' and 'BAG225043: Cameroun 1958–1959', ICRC Archives, Geneva.
10. Meredith Terretta, 'Cameroonian nationalists go global: From forest maquis to a pan-African Accra', Journal of African History, no. 51, 2010, pp. 189–212.
11. Cited in Bureau de documentation du haut commissariat, 'Note sur la situation politique au Cameroun', March 1959, p. 3, CAOM Aff-Pol 3327.
12. Cited in Jean Adalaba, 'La diplomatie du parti nationaliste de l'Union des populations du Cameroun, 1958–1977', MA thesis, University of Yaoundé 1, 2000, p. 35.
13. Max Clos, interview with Ahmadou Ahidjo, Le Figaro, 8–9 August 1959.
14. 'Bulletin de renseignement hebdomadaire du 11 au 17 juin 1959, région Bamiléké', SHD 6H/255.
15. Letter from Colonel du Crest de Villeneuve to General Le Puloch, with annotations by the latter, 12 December 1958, SHD 6H/266.
16. 'Note de service n° 345 de l'escadron de Dschang', Gendarmerie nationale report, Dschang, 25 September 1959, APO PVGNC.
17. 'Bulletin de renseignement hebdomadaire, du 27 septembre au 3 octobre 1959', SHD 6H/255.
18. See Francis Kuikoua, 'Femmes au maquis en région Bamiléké, 1955–1971', MA thesis, University of Yaoundé 1, 2004; Meredith Terretta, 'A miscarriage of revolution: Cameroonian women and nationalism', Stichproben. Wiener Zeitschrift für kritische Afrikastudien, vol. 7, no. 12, 2007 (available at univie.ac.at); and Henry Kam Kah, 'Women's resistance in Cameroon's Western Grassfields: The power of symbols, organization, and leadership, 1957–1961', African Studies Quarterly, vol. 12, no. 3, Summer 2011.
19. Meredith Terretta, 'A miscarriage of revolution', p. 85.

20. 'Plan de défense intérieure du Cameroun', 5 November 1957, SHD 6H/239, 1-14-1, S7302164.

21. See Hemley Boum, *Les Maquisards*, Ciboure 2015; Max Lobe, *Confidences*, Carouge/Geneva 2016. Also worth noting is Jean-Marie Teno's documentary focused on the tragic fate of Ernest Ouandié's daughter: 'Une feuille dans le vent', Les Films du raphia, 2013.

22. For instance, Félix Moumié used the word 'genocide' in his speech to the UN's Fourth Committee (on decolonisation) on 28 October 1958; see Abraham Ngueukam-Tientcheu, 'Les stratégies coloniales de lutte contre les mouvements nationalistes africains: Cas de l'Union des populations du Cameroun (UPC)', PhD thesis, University of Paris 8, 1980, p. 457.

23. Félix-Roland Moumié, Ernest Ouandié and Abel Kingué, *Position de l'UPC vis-à-vis de l'indépendance du Kamerun*, Conakry 1959.

5. Total War (1960–61)

1. Maurice Couve de Murville/Michel Debré correspondence, Archives historiques de Sciences Po, Fonds Couve de Murville, CM7 1960.

2. Michel Debré, *Trois républiques pour une France. Mémoires*, vol. 3: *Gouverner, 1958–1962*, Paris 1988, pp. 336–7.

3. Max Olivier-Lacamp, 'Terrorisme au Cameroun', *Le Figaro*, 23 March 1960.

4. Pierre Talla, 'Un pasteur bamiléké raconte son évasion. Déposition reçue à Bafoussam le 29 avril 1960'; cited in Jean Keller, 'La révolte au pays bamiléké et l'Église', talk in Marseille in 1964, Archives de la Société des missions évangéliques de Paris, DEFAP.

5. Lieutenant-Colonel René Gribelin, 'Situation dans le département Bamiléké', 10 January 1961, pp. 10–11, CADN FAFC/62.

6. Daniel Galland, 'Déchirant Cameroun!', *Réforme*, 27 February 1960.

7. 'PV de la séance de l'Assemblée des combattants, upécistes et Udefec, tenue à Maingui le 5 septembre 1960'; reproduced in 'Bulletin de renseignement hebdomadaire du GTN du 12 au 18 octobre 1960', p. 2, ANY 1AA/158.

8. General Max Briand, 'Rapport sur les opérations militaires au Cameroun en 1960', 7 April 1961, SHD 6H/240.

9. André Blanchet, 'Le Cameroun 1962: Pacification et réunification', talk delivered to the Groupe d'études des problèmes africains, Centre d'étude de politique étrangère, 26 October 1962, pp. 7–8, private archives of André Blanchet, Académie des sciences d'outre-mer.

10. Max Olivier-Lacamp, 'Terrorisme au Cameroun'.

11. Jean Lamberton, 'Les Bamiléké dans le Cameroun d'aujourd'hui', *Revue de défense nationale*, March 1960, pp. 460–77.

12. Jean Evina, 'Rapport de sûreté du 16 au 30 novembre 1960', 1 October 1960, ANY 1AA/158.

13. Cited in René Gribelin, 'Bulletin de renseignement hebdomadaire n° 38 du GTN, du 12 au 18 octobre 1960', p. 2, ANY 1AA/158.

14. 'Note de synthèse de l'ambassadeur [Bénard] au Cameroun au ministère des affaires étrangères et à Jacques Foccart, secrétaire des affaires africaines à l'Elysée', 17 February 1962; cited in Gaëlle Leroy and Valérie Osouf, 'Cameroun: Autopsie d'une indépendance' (documentary), Program 33, 2007.

15. Philippe Nourry, 'J'ai vu les Haoussa, l'arc bandé, monter la garde aux quatre coins du quartier bamiléké', *Le Figaro*, 10 February 1960.

16. 'Note de l'ambassadeur Jean-Pierre Bénard à Jacques Foccart', 2 March 1962, CARAN, Fonds Foccart, FPU 466.

17. Jacques Rousseau, 'Mémoires', unpublished MS, pp. 3–4.

18. Letter addressed to 'Mon cher Maurice', 17 January 1960, CARAN, Fonds Foccart, FPR 151.

19. Authors' interview with Colonel Paul-Théodore Ndjock, Makak, 5 March 2008.

20. Authors' interview with Colonel Sylvestre Mang, Yaoundé, 13 February 2008.

21. Authors' interview with General Pierre Semengue, Yaoundé, 21 December 2007.

22. Authors' interview with Francis Huré, Neuilly-sur-Seine, 15 October 2008.

23. See Pélagie Chantal Belomo Essono, 'L'ordre et la sécurité publics dans la construction de l'État du Cameroun', PhD thesis, École doctorale de science politique de Bordeaux, 2007; and Célestin Christian Tsala Tsala, 'Les détenus politiques au Cameroun de 1958 à 1991', PhD thesis, University of Yaoundé, 2011.

24. TV interview with Ernest Ouandié for Radio Télévision Suisse, *Continents sans visa*, 8 November 1960; available at rts.ch.

25. Authors' interview with Jacques Rousseau, Paris, 6 February 2008.

26. 'The French presence in Cameroon', 26 April 1963, TNA FO 371-167380.

6. Administering Terror

1. Report from Colonel Jean-Victor Blanc, head of the armed forces of the French military mission, 1 April 1963, Mismil Zom 2, Ministry of the Armed Forces, 1962–63, Dossier 1, SHD, 6H271.

2. Milo Report no. 13, 'Summary of the present terrorism in Cameroun Republic', 13 July 1961, TNA FO 371-155342, Internal Security Situation, p. 4.

3. 'PV de la réunion du comité de campagne psychologique auprès des masses du département du Mungo', 4 October 1966, ANY 1AA/24.

4. Edward R. Warner, 'Arrests following the murder of deputy Mopen Noé', 17 September 1963, TNA FO 371-167400.

5. 'Lettre du directeur de la sûreté au secrétaire général de la présidence de la République fédérale du Cameroun', 15 December 1965, ANY 1AA366/1.

6. 'Rapport au directeur de la sûreté fédérale', no. 31/CL/SF, 6 February 1967, pp. 2, 5, ANB; and Fuimu N. Kari, assistant secretary II, 'An analysis of the causes of the Tombel disturbances on 31 December 1966', Pc/f 1966/3, p. 11, ANB.

7. Authors' interview with Félix Sabal Lecco, Yaoundé, 6 December 2007.

8. Jean-Pierre Bénard to the Ministry of Foreign Affairs (MAE), 'Impressions du pays bamiléké', 8 May 1962, CARAN, FPU 466.

9. 'Stage d'information sur le renseignement et l'action civique de Nkongsamba', October 1967, personal archives of Colonel Amos Wanyaka.

10. Cited in Alain d'Aix and Jean-Claude Burger, 'Contre-censure: Main basse sur le Cameroun' (documentary), Inform'Action Films, Quebec 1976 (see informactionfilms.com).

11. Pasma Ngbayou Moluh, 'Le Centre de rééducation civique de Mantoum (1962–1975)', MA thesis, University of Yaoundé 1, 2005, Annexe 6.

12. 'Lettre de l'ambassadeur Jean-Pierre Bénard au ministère des affaires étrangères', 23 March 1962, CARAN FPU 466.

13. 'Possibilités et activités de propagande anti-rebelles des forces', in 'Stage d'information sur le renseignement et l'action civique de Nkongsamba', October 1967, personal archives of Colonel Amos Wanyaka.

14. Ahmadou Ahidjo, 'Discours d'inauguration du village-pionnier de Pitoa', Langui, 18 January 1967; reproduced in Ahmadou Ahidjo, *Anthologie des discours, 1957–1979*, Yaoundé 1980, p. 721.

15. Meredith Terretta, 'Human rights, revolutionary humanitarianism, and African liberation in 1970: Unsettling discontinuities in human rights history', *Humanity*, vol. 14, no. 1, Spring 2023.

16. ORTF, 'Voyage du président Pompidou au Gabon', *Journal de 20 heures*, 12 February 1971; available at ina.fr.

17. Richard Joseph, ed., *Gaullist Africa: Cameroon under Ahmadu Ahidjo*, Enugu 2002 [1978], p. 16.

18. Andrew Larkin, 'Fear of black planet: Paternalism, private industry and profit motives in French development aid to Cameroon, 1946–1974',

University of Minnesota Digital Conservancy, 28 February 2012; available at purl.umn.edu.

19. Joseph, ed., *Gaullist Africa*, p. 32.

20. Ndiva Kofele-Kale, 'Cameroon and its foreign relations', *African Affairs*, vol. 80, no. 319, April 1981, p. 202.

21. Bernard Gauthier and Albert Zeufack, 'Governance and oil revenues in Cameroon', OxCarre Research Paper 29, Oxford University, 7 October 2009, p. 19; available at economics.ox.ac.uk.

22. 'La confession de Le Floch-Prigent', *L'Express*, 12 December 1996.

23. See Jean-Bruno Tagne, 'Cameroun, un silence qui tue', *La Revue du crieur*, no. 23, 2023; 'With or against us: People of the North-West region of Cameroon caught between the army, armed separatists and militias', Amnesty International, 4 July 2023. On the similarities with the 1950–60s war, see Jacob Tatsitsa, 'Des maquisards aux ambaboys: Dette impayée des francophones envers les anglophones', *Journal of the African Literature Association*, vol. 14, no. 2, 2020.

Epilogue: A Stubborn Past, an Impatient Future

1. 'La France au Cameroun (1945–71) – Rapport du volet Recherche de la Commission franco-camerounaise', ed. Karine Ramondy, 28 January 2025, available at vie-publique.fr. 'Les funérailles de la Mémoire. Saison culturelle 2025/2026 – Rapport du volet Artistique de la Commission franco-camerounaise', ed. Blick Bassy, 28 January 2025, available at vie-publique.fr.

2. 'Le rapport Stora vu par deux historiens algériens: "La vérité n'est pas là où il y a l'Etat"', *Mediapart*, 29 January 2021.

3. See Thomas Borrel, Amzat Boukari Yabara, Benoît Collombat and Thomas Deltombe, eds, *Une histoire de la Françafrique: L'empire qui ne veut pas mourir*, Paris 2023 [2021].

Index